CHINESE CONVERSATIONS FOR BEGINNERS

Effective Mandarin Learning with
Authentic Conversational Chinese Dialogues

Chinese Short Stories

Bilingual Book
Chinese • Pinyin • English

LingLing

www.linglingmandarin.com

ACKNOWLEDGEMENTS

I would like to express my sincere thanks to my Chinese friends and colleagues: Hailing Hua, Cathay Zhou, and Dongjie Li, who collaborated with me to complete the Chinese audio for this book.

Special thanks go to my husband Phil, who motivated my creation and assisted with the editing and proofreading the book.

My gratitude also goes to my wonderful students, who study Mandarin with me. You have inspired my writing and have given me valuable feedback to complete this book. Your support is deeply appreciated!

Access FREE Audio!

Check the "Access Audio" chapter
for full instructions.

TABLE OF CONTENTS

INTRODUCTION

ABOUT THE BOOK

Are you a beginner Mandarin learner looking to improve your spoken Chinese in the most effective way possible? If your answer is YES – this book is for you! The book is designed to immerse you in realistic daily conversations in modern China by natives at an appropriate level for learning.

The level of this book is elementary, covering essential topics such as: how to introduce yourself and others; inviting friends out and socializing; ordering food; checking in at hotels; visiting the doctor; taking the metro and ordering a taxi; opening a bank account; renting an apartment; buying everyday essentials; and much more.

China has changed a lot in recent years. The language is ever-evolving, and technology has revolutionized daily interactions. Modern China is more dynamic than ever, affecting lifestyle, language, and culture. It is unsurprising then that many existing books on the market are now impractical and out-of-date. This book presents you with up-to-date vocabulary and phrases, connects you to the lively and authentic language used by natives, and exposes you to multiple aspects of modern life in China, such as the impact of technology in everyday life. It also includes cultural insights and fun stores to enrich your learning experience.

HOW THE BOOK WILL HELP YOU

This book contains 30 conversations that are structured to guide and assist your learning at this stage of your journey. All of the Chinese audio is recorded by native Chinese speakers. The conversations are based in modern China, following consistent storylines and touching on many different topics to give you broad exposure to daily life and interactions in modern-day China. Dialogues consist of:

- Bilingual Chinese-English version (with Pinyin romanization).

- Learning tips to enhance your understanding of the vocabulary and the cultural context of the conversation

- Key vocabulary list to help you to learn and review.

- Chinese only version of the dialogue for self-assessment, to challenge yourself, and to reinforce your learning.

- Highlighted key words and phrases to ease learning

The English translation of the dialogue is not directly word for word; this type of direct translation does not often create an accurate or helpful translation, especially for learning purposes. However, the translation attempts to maintain the original meaning while aiming for a natural reading in English, where possible. Significant cultural differences also affect how people address one another and interact; this, in addition to fundamental differences between the Chinese and English languages and their usage in everyday speech, may result in some sentences appearing slightly strange at first. Do not fear, as you will become accustomed to this through increased exposure to the culture and language. One of the objectives of this book is to do precisely that by allowing you to read and listen in your own time and by providing helpful hints along the way.

Most characters and vocabulary in this book are chosen from HSK elementary levels 1 and 2, with some from level 3. The book also includes many new words and phrases used in the modern internet era. If you are studying Chinese towards an HSK qualification, this book will help you review and reinforce what you have learned through classes or textbooks in a practical and fun way. If you are a general learner, this book helps you to master essential daily vocabulary, phrases, and sentence patterns through exposure to their usage in realistic conversations.

FREE AUDIO!

Great news – the audio for the book is a FREE gift. Don't forget to check the instructions in the "Access Audio" chapter for how to access it! The audio includes all 30 Chinese conversations recorded by native Chinese speakers!

LEARN CHINESE WITH A NEW VISION

Do you know that Chinese is the second most spoken language in the world? With over 1 billion speakers in China and all over the globe, right after English. China is also a rising global superpower with the second-largest economy predicted to become the largest within the next decade. Mastering the Chinese language opens a world of possibilities, opportunities, and potential for you!

Chinese is also an incredibly varied, dynamic, artistic, and fascinating language. Studying Chinese is not just about learning a great language but also exploring a different way of thinking, experiencing new perspectives, understanding a rich culture developed over thousands of years, and finding peace and balance in a lifelong beneficial learning experience.

How to Learn Chinese: Tips from LingLing

Dear readers, thank you for purchasing this first book in my Spoken Chinese series! I hope this book serves you well to expand your vocabulary, equip you with authentic native phrases, and provide you with unique insights to better understand the Chinese language and culture to become a confident and effective Chinese speaker.

Become an Effective Learner

In Chinese, we have a well-known idiom 事半功倍 (shì bàn gōng bèi) (get twice the result with half the effort). You can cut short a long process with an effective learning method. It may seem obvious, the best way to learn Chinese is to use it as often as possible. Like any skill, the more you practice, the more it will become second nature, like muscle memory.

Make the most of each dialogue in the book by paying attention to the language flow and keep **reading it aloud** until you can read it naturally and fluently - even imagining yourself in the situation and acting it out. Use the accompanying audio to help by imitating the accent and expression of the people in the audio. And of course, with Chinese being a tonal language, listen carefully for the pronunciation and tones of each word. I suggest you follow this process:

1. Go through the bilingual version of each conversation to identify the new words and phrases in context, referring to the Key Vocabulary list for their definitions when unsure.

2. Listen to the audio while following the text to pick up the correct pronunciation - pause and rewind if necessary.

3. Practice by reading the text aloud until you can read out the entire dialogue fluently. Pay attention to the transitional words and phrases to master the authentic language flow.

4. Head to the Chinese version of the dialogue, test yourself by reading it out without the help of pinyin and English. Mastering Chinese on its own is the key to leveling up.

5. Return to the conversation audio, test yourself by listening to it without the help of the text. If you miss some parts, go back to check with the text. Keep practicing until you can comprehend with the audio alone.

REVIEW AND PRACTICE

Repetition is the mother of learning! Make sure you go back to each dialogue and review the vocabularies frequently, and find a language partner to practice and rehearse the conversations through role-playing if possible. The more you review and practice, the better your Mandarin will be!

BE YOUR OWN CREATOR

You become a true master through creation and application! Apply the vocabularies, phrases, and sentence patterns you learned from each dialogue to your own conversations, whether in real-life practice or imaginary scenarios. Remember - the ultimate goal of learning Mandarin is to effectively communicate and understand the language in your own experiences. You can only achieve this by applying what you have learned in practice!

BELIEVE IN YOURSELF

Believe in yourself and have confidence! Never be afraid of making mistakes. In real life, even advanced learners and native speakers make mistakes! Plus, mistakes only make us grow quicker! So, never let mistakes put you off. Instead, be bold, embrace and learn from mistakes! Remember, success and achievement come from confidence, perseverance, and a never-give-up attitude! Just like the famous Chinese idiom:

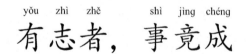

yǒu   zhì   zhě   shì   jìng   chéng

有志者，事竟成

Nothing is Impossible to a Willing Heart

我 叫 杰 明
wǒ jiào jié míng

MY NAME IS JAMIE

杰明：你好！我叫杰明。请问，你叫什么？
jié míng nǐ hǎo wǒ jiào jié míng qǐng wèn nǐ jiào shén me

Jamie: Hello! I am Jamie. **May I ask**, what's your name?

李丽：你好！我叫李丽。你是美国人吗？
lǐ lì nǐ hǎo wǒ jiào lǐ lì nǐ shì měi guó rén ma

Li Li: Hello! I am Li Li. Are you **American**?

杰明：不是，我是英国人。
jié míng bù shì wǒ shì yīng guó rén

Jamie: No, I am British.

李丽："杰明"是你的中文名字吗？
lǐ lì jié míng shì nǐ de zhōng wén míng zì ma

Li Li: Is "Jié Míng" your **Chinese name**?

杰明：是的。我的英文名字是 Jamie, 姓 Green。
jié míng shì de wǒ de yīng wén míng zì shì xìng

Jamie: Yes. My **English name** is Jamie and my **surname** is Green.

李丽：我也有英文名字，叫 Lily。
lǐ lì wǒ yě yǒu yīng wén míng zì jiào

Li Li: I **also** have an English name, called Lily.

杰明：这是很好的英文名字！
jié míng zhè shì hěn hǎo de yīng wén míng zì

Jamie: This is a **very good** English name!

李丽：哪里哪里！你是**大学生**吗？
Li Li: Thank you for your compliment! Are you a **University student**?

杰明：是的。
Jamie: Yes.

李丽：这是你**第一次**来中国吗？
Li Li: Is this your **first time** coming to China?

杰明：对，我**上个星期**才到中国。
Jamie: Yes, I only arrived **last week**.

李丽：中国很大，你**为什么**会**选择**上海？
Li Li: China is very big, **why** do you **choose** Shanghai?

杰明：**因为**上海很**有名**，而且我在上海有很多中国
朋友。
Jamie: **Because** Shanghai is very **famous**, plus I have many Chinese **friends** in
Shanghai.

李丽：那你的中文**怎么样**？
Li Li: So, **how** is your Chinese?

杰明：**一般般**。我在英国学了几年，现在**打算**在中国
再学**半年**。
Jamie: It's **average**. I studied it in the UK for a few years, and now I **plan to**
study for another **half year** in China.

李丽：你**觉得**学中文**难**吗？
Li Li: Do you **think** it is **hard** to learn Chinese?

杰明：**有一点儿**难，**特别**是写汉字。
Jamie: **A little** hard, **especially** writing Chinese characters.

李丽：如果你用**拼音打字**，就不难。
Li Li: If you **type in Pinyin**, it's not hard.

jié míng　duì　　dàn shì　wǒ hěn　xǐ huān liàn xí　xiě hàn zì　　　wǒ jué dé hàn zì hěn měi

杰明：对！但是我很**喜欢**练习写汉字，我觉得汉字很**美**。

Jamie: Correct! But I **like to** practice writing Chinese. I think Chinese characters are very **beautiful**.

lǐ　lì　　shì　ā　　wǒ de hěn duō wài guó péng yǒu yě zhè yàngshuō　zhù nǐ hǎo yùn

李丽：是啊！我的很多**外国**朋友也这样说。**祝你好运！**

Li Li: Indeed! Many of my **foreign** friends also said the same to me. **Good luck to you!**

jié míng　xiè xie nǐ　　hěn gāo xīng rèn shí nǐ

杰明：谢谢你！很高兴**认识**你！

Jamie: Thank you! Nice to **meet** you!

lǐ　lì　　wǒ yě hěn gāo xīng rèn shí nǐ　　zài jiàn

李丽：我**也**很高兴认识你！**再见！**

Li Li: Nice to meet you **too**! **Goodbye!**

jié míng　zài jiàn

杰明：再见

Jamie: Goodbye!

Learning Tip

nǎ　　lǐ　　nǎ　　lǐ
哪 里 哪 里 literally translates to "where, where," but it is a colloquial term used to show modesty in acknowledging a compliment.

Key Vocabulary

qǐng wèn 请 问	v.	excuse me/ may I ask	míng zì 名 字	n.	name
xìng 姓	n.	surname	dì yī cì 第 一 次	n.	first time
xīng qī 星 期	n.	week	xuǎn zé 选 择	v.	to choose
wèi shén me 为 什 么	adv.	why	yīn wèi 因 为	conj.	because
yǒu míng 有 名	adj.	famous	yī bān bān 一 般 般	adj.	average
dǎ suàn 打 算	v.	to plan	nán 难	adj.	hard (difficult)
pīn yīn dǎ zì 拼 音 打 字		type pinyin	xǐ huān 喜 欢	v.	to like
wài guó 外 国	n.	foreign country	zhù nǐ hǎo yùn 祝 你 好 运	vp.	wish you good luck

Chinese Version

杰明：你好！我叫杰明。请问，你叫什么？

李丽：你好！我叫李丽。你是美国人吗？

杰明：不是，我是英国人。

李丽：杰明是你的中文名字吗？

杰明：是的。我的英文名字是 Jamie，姓Green。

李丽：我也有英文名字，叫Lily。

杰明：这是很好的英文名字！

李丽：哪里哪里！你是大学生吗？

杰明：是的。

李丽：这是你第一次来中国吗？

杰明：对，我上个星期才到中国。

李丽：中国很大，你为什么会选择上海？

杰明：因为上海很有名，而且我在上海有很多中国朋友。

李丽：那你的中文怎么样？

杰明：一般般。我在英国学了几年，现在打算在中国再学半年。

李丽：你觉得学中文难吗？

杰明：有一点儿难，特别是写汉字。

李丽：如果你用拼音打字，就不难。

杰明：对！但是我很喜欢练习写汉字，我觉得汉字很美。

李丽：是啊！我的很多外国朋友也这样说。祝你好运！

杰明：谢谢你！很高兴认识你！

李丽：我也很高兴认识你！再见！

杰明：再见！

2 我的朋友，苏飞

wǒ de péng yǒu sū fēi

MY FRIEND, SU FEI

jié míng zǎo shàng hǎo   lǐ lì
杰明：早 上 好！李丽。
Jamie: Good **morning**, Li Li!

lǐ lì   zǎo   jīn tiān zěn me yàng
李丽：早！今天 怎么样？
Li Li: Morning! How are you **today**?

jié míng hái kě yǐ   nǐ ne
杰明：还可以！你呢？
Jamie: Not bad! **What about you**?

lǐ lì   jīn tiān yǒu diǎn ér lèi   yīn wèi gōng zuò tài máng le
李丽：今天有点儿累，因为工作太忙了。
Li Li: I am a bit **tired** today, because my **work** has been too **busy**.

jié míng nǐ zài nǎ lǐ gōng zuò
杰明：你在哪里工作？
Jamie: **Where** do you work?

lǐ lì   zài zhōng guó yín háng   lí zhè lǐ bù yuǎn   nǐ kàn   nà shì shéi
李丽：在 中国 银行，离这里不远。你看，那是谁？
Li Li: At the **Bank** of China, not **far** from here. Look, **who's** that?

jié míng nà shì sū fēi   shì wǒ de hǎo péng yǒu   sū fēi   wǒ zài zhè ér
杰明：那是苏飞，是我的好朋友。苏飞，我在这儿。
Jamie: That's Su Fei, my **good friend**. Su Fei, I am **here**.

苏飞走过来...
sū fēi zǒu guò lái

Su Fei arriving...

杰明：苏飞，这是我的**新朋友**，叫李丽。
jié míng sū fēi zhè shì wǒ de xīn péng yǒu jiào lǐ lì

Jamie: Su Fei, this is my **new friend**, Li Li.

苏飞：你好！我叫苏飞。
sū fēi nǐ hǎo wǒ jiào sū fēi

Su Fei: Hello! My name is Su Fei.

李丽：你好！我和杰明**经常**来这里喝**咖啡**，后来就认识了。
lǐ lì nǐ hǎo wǒ hé jié míng jīng cháng lái zhè lǐ hē kā fēi hòu lái jiù rèn shí le

Li Li: Hello! Jamie and I **often** come here to drink **coffee**, and we got to know each other.

杰明：是啊！我刚刚在**等**你的时候，又**遇到**李丽了。
jié míng shì ā wǒ gānggāng zài děng nǐ de shí hòu yòu yù dào lǐ lì le

Jamie: Indeed! When I was **waiting** for you, I **bumped into** Li Li again.

苏飞：杰明就是个**咖啡大王**！李丽，你也**喜欢**喝咖啡吗？
sū fēi jié míng jiù shì gè kā fēi dà wáng lǐ lì nǐ yě xǐ huān hē kā fēi ma

Su Fei: Jamie is a **coffee lover** (coffee king)! Li Li, do you **like** coffee too?

李丽：一般般，我**更**喜欢喝茶，但是**附近**没有茶馆。
lǐ lì yī bān bān wǒ gèng xǐ huān hē chá dàn shì fù jìn méi yǒu chá guǎn

Li Li: Just so so, I like tea **more**, but there is no tea house **nearby**.

苏飞：我也是。**对了**，你是上海人吗？
sū fēi wǒ yě shì duì le nǐ shì shàng hǎi rén ma

Su Fei: Me too. **By the way**, are you from Shanghai?

李丽：不是，我是四川人。
lǐ lì bù shì wǒ shì sì chuān rén

Li Li: No, I am from Sichuan.

苏飞：四川很**有名**，川菜也很**好吃**！
sū fēi sì chuān hěn yǒu míng chuān cài yě hěn hǎo chī

Su Fei: Sichuan is very **famous** and Sichuan cuisine is also very **delicious**!

李丽：是啊！你**去过**四川吗？
lǐ lì shì ā nǐ qù guò sì chuān ma

Li Li: Yes! **Have** you **been** to Sichuan?

7

sū fēi qù guò wǒ qù le chéng dū zuì xǐ huān nà lǐ de měi shí
苏飞：去过。我**去了**成都，最喜欢那里的**美食**！
Su Fei: Yes. I **went to** Chengdu and really loved the **delicacies** there!

lǐ lì nà nǐ qù chī huǒ guō le ma
李丽：那你去吃**火锅**了吗？
Li Li: So, did you eat **hot pot**?

sū fēi dāng rán qù le sì tiān jiù chī le liǎng cì huǒ guō
苏飞：**当然**！去了四天就吃了**两次**火锅！
Su Fei: Of course! I ate hot pot **twice** in four days!

jié míng wā kàn lái nǐ shì gè huǒ guō dà wáng
杰明：哇！**看来**，你是个**火锅大王**。
Jamie: Wow! **It seems** that you are a **Hot Pot Lover** (hot pot king).

Learning Tip

dà wáng
大王 literally means "big king," it is a colloquial term used to refer to someone who is a big fan or lover of something.

Key Vocabulary

zěn me yàng 怎 么 样	*pro.*	how	lèi 累	*adj.*	tired
máng 忙	*adj.*	busy	gōng zuò 工 作	*v.* *n.*	to work work
yín háng 银 行	*n.*	bank	péng yǒu 朋 友	*n.*	friend
xīn 新	*adj.*	new	jīng cháng 经 常	*adj.*	often
kā fēi 咖 啡	*n.*	coffee	děng 等	*v.*	to wait
yù dào 遇 到	*v.*	to encounter	chá guǎn 茶 馆	*n.*	tea house
měi shí 美 食	*n.*	delicacy	hǎo chī 好 吃	*adj.*	delicious
duì le 对 了	*interj.*	similar to "oh yes" or "by the way"	huǒ guō 火 锅	*n.*	hotpot

Chinese Version

杰明：早上好！李丽。
李丽：早！今天怎么样？
杰明：还可以！你呢？
李丽：今天有点儿累，因为工作太忙了。
杰明：你在哪里工作？
李丽：在中国银行，离这里不远。你看，那是谁？
杰明：那是苏飞，是我的好朋友。苏飞，我在这儿。

苏飞走过来…

杰明：苏飞，这是我的新朋友，叫李丽。
苏飞：你好！我叫苏飞。
李丽：你好！我和杰明经常来这里喝咖啡，后来就认识了。
杰明：是啊！我刚刚在等你的时候，又遇到李丽了。
苏飞：杰明就是个咖啡大王！李丽，你也喜欢喝咖啡吗？
李丽：一般般，我更喜欢喝茶，但是附近没有茶馆。
苏飞：我也是。对了，你是上海人吗？
李丽：不是，我是四川人。
苏飞：四川很有名，川菜也很好吃！
李丽：是啊！你去过四川吗？
苏飞：去过。我去了成都，最喜欢那里的美食！
李丽：那你去吃火锅了吗？
苏飞：当然！去了四天就吃了两次火锅！
杰明：哇！看来，你是个火锅大王。

3

我太忙了
wǒ tài máng le

I Am Too Busy

sū fēi   nǐ xiǎng qù nǎ ér
苏飞:你 想 去 哪 儿?
Su Fei: Where do you **want to** go?

jié míng wǒ xiǎng qù chāo shì mǎi dōng xī   nǐ yào gēn wǒ qù ma
杰明:我 想 去 超市 买 东西,你 要 跟 我 去 吗?
Jamie: I want to go to the **supermarket** to buy things, would you like to go **with** me?

sū fēi   hǎo ba   wǒ yě yào qù mǎi wǔ fàn
苏飞:好 吧,我 也 要 去 买 午饭。
Su Fei: Okay, I want to buy **lunch** too.

jié míng jīn tiān máng ma
杰明:今 天 忙 吗?
Jamie: Are you **busy** today?

sū fēi   tài máng le   yě kuài lèi chéng gǒu le
苏飞:太 忙 了,也 快 累 成 狗 了!
Su Fei: Too busy, and **extremely tired** (as tired as a dog)!

jié míng wéi shén me
杰明:为 什 么?
Jamie: Why?

sū fēi   wǒ jīn tiān zǎo shàngcóng bā diǎn jiù kāi shǐ shàng bān   yī huì ér hái yào
苏飞:我 今 天 早 上 从 八 点 就 开 始 上 班,一 会 儿 还 要
huí bàn gōng shì kāi huì
回 办 公 室 开 会。

Su Fei: I started **working** at 8 o'clock this morning, and have to go back to the **office** for a meeting later.

jié míng   nǐ zěn me   nà me   zǎo shàng bān
杰明：你 怎 么 **那 么 早** 上 班？
Jamie: Why did you start work **so early**?

sū fēi   jīn tiān de gōng zuò tài duō le   pà zuò bù wán
苏飞：今 天 的 **工 作** 太 多 了，**怕** 做 不 完。
Su Fei: I have too much **work** today and I'm **afraid** I cannot finish it.

jié míng   wéi shén me dān xīn zuò bù wán
杰明：为 什 么 **担 心** 做 不 完？
Jamie: Why do you **worry** about it?

sū fēi   yīn wèi   jīn tiān xià wǔ   jīng lǐ yào hé wǒ men kāi huì   yào kāi sān gè
苏飞：因 为，今 天 **下 午**，**经 理** 要 和 我 们 **开 会**，要 开 三 个
xiǎo shí
小 时。
Su Fei: Because, this **afternoon** the **manager** will **have a meeting** with us, for 3 **hours**.

jié míng   nà me cháng shí jiān   nǐ men jīng lǐ   shì gè huà duō de rén ma
杰明：那 么 长 **时 间**！你 们 经 理 是 个 **话 多** 的 人 吗？
Jamie: Such a long **time**! Is your manager a **talkative** person?

sū fēi   dāng rán   ér qiě zǒng shì shuō yī xiē méi yòng de huà
苏飞：**当 然**！**而 且** 总 是 说 一 些 **没 用** 的 话！
Su Fei: Of course! **Plus** always speaks **useless** things!

jié míng   rú guǒ tā làng fèi nǐ men de shí jiān   jiù shì gè méi yòng de jīng lǐ
杰明：**如 果** 他 **浪 费** 你 们 的 时 间，就 是 个 没 用 的 经 理。
Jamie: **If** he **wastes** your time, he is a useless manager.

sū fēi   shì ā   hěn duō tóng shì yě shuō tā méi yòng
苏飞：是 啊！很 多 **同 事** 也 说 他 没 用！
Su Fei: Indeed! Many **colleagues** also say he is useless!

jié míng   nà nǐ men jīng cháng hé jīng lǐ kāi huì ma
杰明：那 你 们 **经 常** 和 经 理 开 会 吗？
Jamie: Do you **often** have meetings with the manager?

sū fēi   ng   yī zhōu yī cì   yī bān shì xīng qī èr xià wǔ
苏飞：嗯，**一 周 一 次**，**一 般** 是 星 期 二 下 午。
Su Fei: Well, **once a week**, **usually** on Tuesday afternoon.

jié míng   āi   nǐ zhēn dǎo méi   nà nǐ jīn tiān shén me shí hòu xià bān
杰明：唉！你 真 **倒 霉**！那 你 今 天 **什 么 时 候** 下 班。
Jamie: Ugh! You are so **unlucky**! Then **when** will you finish work today?

苏飞：我 也 不 知 道，**可 能** 是 七 点 。
sū fēi wǒ yě bù zhī dào kě néng shì qī diǎn

Su Fei: I don't know, **maybe** seven o'clock.

杰明：那 我 七 点 去 你 的 **公 司** 门 口 **等** 你，我 们 一 起 吃 **晚**
jié míng nà wǒ qī diǎn qù nǐ de gōng sī mén kǒu děng nǐ wǒ men yī qǐ chī wǎn

饭，好 吗？
fàn hǎo ma

Jamie: Then I will go to your **company** gate to **wait for** you at seven o'clock. Let's have **dinner** together, OK?

苏飞：好 。我 想 吃 **炒饭**，你 呢？
sū fēi hǎo wǒ xiǎng chī chǎo fàn nǐ ne

Su Fei: OK. I want to eat **fried rice**, what about you?

杰明：我 也 想 吃 炒饭 。
jié míng wǒ yě xiǎng chī chǎo fàn

Jamie: Me too.

Learning Tip

累 成 狗 means "as tired as a dog." This
lèi chéng gǒu

commonly used slang expression evokes the image of an exhausted dog lying on the ground with mouth wide open, tongue out, and panting heavily.

Key Vocabulary

nǎ ér 哪儿	*pro.*	where	chāo shì 超市	*n.*	supermarket
shàng bān 上班	*v.*	to go to work/ start work	xià bān 下班	*v.*	to get off work/ finish work
bàn gōng shì 办公室	*n.*	office	nà me 那么	*pro.*	so
pà 怕	*adj.* *v.*	afraid to fear	dān xīn 担心	*adj.* *v.*	worried to worry
jīng lǐ 经理	*n.*	manager	kāi huì 开会	*v.*	to have a meeting
huà duō 话多	*adj.*	talkative	méi yòng 没用	*adj.*	useless
làng fèi 浪费	*v.*	to waste	tóng shì 同事	*n.*	colleague
dǎo méi 倒霉	*adj.*	unlucky	kě néng 可能	*adv.*	possibly
gōng sī 公司	*n.*	company	chǎo fàn 炒饭	*n.*	fried rice
wǔ fàn 午饭	*n.*	lunch	wǎn fàn 晚饭	*n.*	dinner

Chinese Version

苏 飞：你想去哪儿？

杰 明：我想去超市买东西,你要跟我去吗？

苏 飞：好吧,我也要去买午饭。

杰 明：今天忙吗？

苏 飞：太忙了,也快累成狗了！

杰 明：为什么？

苏 飞：我今天早上从八点就开始上班,一会儿还要回办公室开会。

杰 明：你怎么那么早上班？

苏 飞：今天的工作太多了,怕做不完。

杰 明：为什么担心做不完？

苏 飞：因为,今天下午,经理要和我们开会,要开三个小时。

杰 明：那么长时间！你们经理是个话多的人吗？

苏 飞：当然！而且总是说一些没用的话！

杰 明：如果他浪费你们的时间,就是个没用的经理。

苏 飞：是啊！很多同事也说他没用！

杰 明：那你们经常和经理开会吗？

苏 飞：嗯,一周一次,一般是星期二下午。

杰 明：唉！你真倒霉！那你今天什么时候下班。

苏 飞：我也不知道,可能是七点。

杰 明：那我七点去你的公司门口等你,我们一起吃晚饭,好吗？

苏 飞：好。我想吃炒饭,你呢？

杰 明：我也想吃炒饭。

我可以加你微信吗？

wǒ kě yǐ jiā nǐ wēi xìn ma

MAY I ADD YOU ON WECHAT?

sū fēi hēi lǐ lì wǒ men yòu jiàn miàn le
苏飞：嗨！李丽，我们又见面了！
Su Fei: **Hi**! Li Li, we **meet** again!

lǐ lì sū fēi zhēn de shì nǐ
李丽：苏飞！真的是你。
Li Li: Su Fei! It **really** is you.

sū fēi shì ā wǒ men shàng xīng qī wǔ zài kā fēi guǎn jiàn guò
苏飞：是啊！我们上星期五在咖啡馆见过。
Su Fei: Yes! We met in the cafe **last Friday**.

lǐ lì nǐ yě zài zhè fù jìn shàng bān ma
李丽：你也在这附近上班吗？
Li Li: Do you also work **nearby**?

sū fēi duì nǐ kàn jiù zài zhōng guó yín háng páng biān de nà zuò lóu
苏飞：对！你看，就在中国银行旁边的那座楼。
Su Fei: Yes! You see, that **building** next to the **Bank of China**.

lǐ lì zhēn de ma wǒ jiù zài zhōng guó yín háng shàng bān
李丽：真的吗？我就在中国银行上班。
Li Li: Really? I am working at the Bank of China.

sū fēi wā tài qiǎo le wǒ zài zhè lǐ gōng zuò bàn nián le zěn me méi jiàn
苏飞：哇！太巧了！我在这里工作半年了，怎么没见
guò nǐ
过你？

Su Fei: Wow! **What a coincidence**! I have been working here for half a year, **why haven't I seen you?**

lǐ lì shì zhè yàng de wǒ shàng gè yuè cái lái yín háng gōng zuò
李丽：是这样的，我上个月才来银行工作。
Li Li: Well, I only came to work in the bank **last month.**

sū fēi ā kàn lái rú guǒ méi yǒu jié míng wǒ men yě hěn kě néng huì yù dào
苏飞：啊！看来，如果没有杰明，我们也很可能会遇到。
Su Fei: Ah! **It seems** even without Jamie, we are **likely to** encounter one another anyway.

lǐ lì méi cuò nà nǐ rèn shí jié míng duō jiǔ le
李丽：没错！那你认识杰明多久了？
Li Li: That's right! So, **how long** have you known Jamie?

sū fēi ng kuài yī nián le wǒ men zài yīng guó de shí hòu jiù rèn shí le
苏飞：嗯，快一年了。我们在英国的时候就认识了。
Su Fei: Um, **almost** a year. We met when we were in the **UK**.

lǐ lì zhēn hǎo duì le wǒ kě yǐ jiā nǐ wēi xìn ma
李丽：真好！对了，我可以加你微信吗？
Li Li: That's great! **By the way**, may I add your **WeChat**?

sū fēi dāng rán kě yǐ wǒ de wēi xìn hào shì
苏飞：当然可以！我的微信号是Sophie93。
Su Fei: Of course! My **WeChat ID** is Sophie93.

lǐ lì hǎo de jiā shàng le
李丽：好的，加上了。
Li Li: OK, just added.

sū fēi nǐ de wēi xìn tóu xiàng zhēn yǒu yì sī
苏飞：你的微信头像真有意思。
Su Fei: Your WeChat **profile picture** is really **interesting**.

lǐ lì ng zhè shì wǒ hé wǒ xiǎo gǒu de zhào piàn
李丽：嗯，这是我和我小狗的照片。
Li Li: Well, this is a **photo** of me and my little dog.

sū fēi tā zhēn kě ài míng tiān zhōng wǔ nǐ yǒu shí jiān ma wǒ men kě yǐ
苏飞：它真可爱！明天中午你有时间吗？我们可以
yī qǐ qù chī wǔ fàn
一起去吃午饭。
Su Fei: He is so **cute**! Will you have time **midday tomorrow**? We can go to have lunch **together**.

lǐ lì kě yǐ ā wǒ zhōng wǔ yī bān diǎn xiū xī nǐ ne
李丽：可以啊！我中午一般12点休息，你呢？
Li Li: Yes! I usually **have a break** at 12 noon, what about you?

苏飞：我也是。
sū fēi   wǒ yě shì

Su Fei: Me too.

李丽：那我们明天12点在银行门口见面吧。
lǐ lì   nà wǒ men míng tiān   diǎn zài yín háng mén kǒu jiàn miàn ba

Li Li: Let's meet at the **gate** of the bank at 12:00 tomorrow.

苏飞：可以！我知道一家很棒的面馆，我带你去。
sū fēi   kě yǐ   wǒ zhī dào yī jiā hěn bàng de miànguǎn   wǒ dài nǐ qù

Su Fei: Great! I **know** a **great** noodle restaurant; I will **take** you there.

李丽：好的！明天见！
lǐ lì   hǎo de   míng tiān jiàn

Li Li: Okay! see you **tomorrow!**

苏飞：明天见！
sū fēi   míng tiān jiàn

Su Fei: See you!

Learning Tip

微信 (wēi xìn) is a hugely popular smartphone app, known internationally as WeChat.

Originally an instant messaging app, it has now evolved into a multipurpose app impacting and shaping almost every aspect of life in China. From instant messaging, social media functions, and gaming, to payment for everyday items (paying for rent, buying groceries, booking train tickets, almost anything can be paid for).

The addition of 小程序 (xiǎo chéng xù) (mini apps) has expanded WeChat's functionality and impact further.

Key Vocabulary

hēi 嗨	*interj.*	hi / hey		jiàn miàn 见面	*v.*	to meet
zhēn 真	*adv.*	really		kā fēi guǎn 咖啡馆	*n.*	cafe
fù jìn 附近	*n.*	nearby		lóu 楼	*n.*	building
yuè 月	*n.*	month		kàn lái 看来	*adv.*	seem
duō jiǔ 多久		how long		kuài 快	*adv.*	almost
wēi xìn 微信	*n.*	WeChat		tóu xiàng 头像	*n.*	profile picture
zhào piàn 照片	*n.*	photo		kě ài 可爱	*adj.*	cute
shí jiān 时间	*n.*	time		xiū xī 休息	*v.*	to rest
mén kǒu 门口	*n.*	gate		bàng 棒	*adj.*	great

Chinese Version

苏飞：嗨!李丽,我们又见面了!

李丽：苏飞!真的是你。

苏飞：是啊!我们上星期五在咖啡馆见过。

李丽：你也在这附近上班吗?

苏飞：对!你看,就在中国银行旁边的那座楼。

李丽：真的吗?我就在中国银行上班。

苏飞：哇!太巧了!我在这里工作半年了,怎么没见过你?

李丽：是这样的,我上个月才来银行工作。

苏飞：啊!看来,如果没有杰明,我们也很可能会遇到。

李丽：没错!那你认识杰明多久了?

苏飞：嗯,快一年了。我们在英国的时候就认识了。

李丽：真好!对了,我可以加你微信吗?

苏飞：当然可以! 我的微信号是Sophie93。

李丽：好的,加上了。

苏飞：你的微信头像真有意思。

李丽：嗯,这是我和我小狗的照片。

苏飞：它真可爱! 明天中午你有时间吗? 我们可以一起去吃午饭。

李丽：可以啊!我中午一般12点休息,你呢?

苏飞：我也是。

李丽：那我们明天12点在银行门口见面吧。

苏飞：可以!我知道一家很棒的面馆,我带你去。

李丽：好的!明天见!

苏飞：明天见!

5

我的兄弟姐妹
wǒ de xiōng dì jiě mèi

MY SIBLINGS

杰明:李丽，**最近**怎么样？
jié míng lǐ lì zuì jìn zěn me yàng

Jamie: Li Li, how are you **recently**?

李丽:**还不错**！你呢？
lǐ lì hái bù cuò nǐ ne

Li Li: **Not bad**! How about you?

杰明:非常好，也非常**开心**！**因为**我妈妈会来**看**我。
jié míng fēi cháng hǎo yě fēi cháng kāi xīn yīn wèi wǒ mā mā huì lái kàn wǒ

Jamie: Very good and very **happy**! **Because** my mum will come to **see** me.

李丽:太好了！她什么时候**到**？
lǐ lì tài hǎo le tā shén me shí hòu dào

Li Li: Great! When will she **arrive**?

杰明:她**下星期五**早上到，我和苏飞会去**飞机场**接她。
jié míng tā xià xīng qī wǔ zǎo shàng dào wǒ hé sū fēi huì qù fēi jī chǎng jiē tā

Jamie: She will arrive **next Friday** morning, Su Fei and I will pick her up at the
airport.

李丽:你爸爸呢？也会**一起**来吗？
lǐ lì nǐ bà bà ne yě huì yī qǐ lái ma

Li Li: What about your dad? Will he come **together** as well?

杰明:不会，我爸爸的工作很忙，**来不了**。
jié míng bù huì wǒ bà bà de gōng zuò hěn máng lái bù liǎo

Jamie: No, my dad is very busy at work, he **can't come**.

lǐ lì duì le nǐ yǒu xiōng dì jiě mèi ma
李丽：对了，你有**兄弟姐妹**吗？
Li Li:　By the way, do you have any **siblings**?

jié míng wǒ yǒu yī gè jiě jie hé liǎng gè gē ge nǐ ne
杰明：我有一个**姐姐**和两个**哥哥**。你呢？
Jamie:　I have one **older sister** and two **older brothers**. What about you?

lǐ lì wǒ yǒu yī gè dì di zài shàng xué
李丽：我有一个**弟弟**，在上学。
Li Li:　I have a **younger brother** in school.

jié míng tā duō dà
杰明：他**多大**？
Jamie:　**How old** is he?

lǐ lì suì le nǐ kàn zhè shì tā de zhàopiàn
李丽：17岁了。你看，这是他的**照片**！
Li Li:　17 years old. Look, this is his **picture**!

jié míng ng nǐ dì di kàn shàng qù hěn shuài
杰明：嗯，你弟弟**看上去**很**帅**！
Jamie:　Well, your brother **looks** very **handsome**!

lǐ lì nǐ de jiě jie hé gē ge ne
李丽：你的姐姐和哥哥呢？
Li Li:　What about your sister and brothers?

jié míng tā men dōu gōng zuò le wǒ de jiě jie shì lǜ shī liǎng gè gē ge dōu shì
杰明：他们**都**工作了。我的姐姐是**律师**，两个哥哥都是
diàn nǎo gōngchéng shī
电脑工程师。
Jamie:　They are **all** working. My older sister is a **lawyer**, and my two older
　　　　brothers are **computer engineers**.

lǐ lì zhēn kù duì le nǐ mā mā jīn nián duō dà
李丽：真**酷**！对了，你妈妈**今年**多大？
Li Li:　That's **cool**! By the way, how old is your mum **this year**?

jié míng wǒ mā mā jīn nián wǔ shí sān suì
杰明：我妈妈今年五十三岁。
Jamie:　My mum is 53 this year.

lǐ lì tā yǐ qián lái guò zhōng guó ma
李丽：她**以前**来过中国吗？
Li Li:　Has she been to China **before**?

jié míng méi yǒu zhè shì dì yī cì suǒ yǐ tā fēi cháng jī dòng
杰明：没有。这是**第一次**！所以她非常**激动**！
Jamie:　No. This is the **first time**! So, she is very **excited**!

lǐ lì   tài hǎo le   zhù nǐ men wán dé kāi xīn
李丽：太好了！祝你们玩得开心！
Li Li: Great! May you **have a great time**!

jié míng xiè xie nǐ
杰明：谢谢你！
Jamie: Thank you!

Key and Supplementary Vocabulary

zuì jìn 最 近	*n.*	recently	kāi xīn 开 心	*adj.*	happy
kàn 看	*v.*	to see	dào 到	*v.*	to arrive
xià 下	*n.*	next	fēi jī chǎng 飞 机 场	*n.*	airport
duō dà 多 大		how old?	shuài 帅	*adj.*	handsome
lǜ shī 律 师	*n.*	lawyer	diàn nǎo 电 脑	*n.*	computer
gōngchéng shī 工 程 师	*n.*	engineer	kù 酷	*adj.*	cool
yǐ qián 以 前	*n.*	before	jī dòng 激 动	*adj.*	excited
yī qǐ 一 起	*adv.*	together	xiōng dì jiě mèi 兄 弟 姐 妹	*n.*	siblings
gē ge 哥 哥	*n.*	older brother	dì di 弟 弟	*n.*	younger brother
jiě jie 姐 姐	*n.*	older sister	mèi mei 妹 妹	*n.*	younger sister
nán péng yǒu 男 朋 友	*n.*	boyfriend	nǚ péng yǒu 女 朋 友	*n.*	girlfriend
lǎo gōng 老 公	*n.*	husband	lǎo pó 老 婆	*n.*	wife
nǚ ér 女 儿	*n.*	daughter	ér zǐ 儿 子	*n.*	son

Chinese Version

杰明：李丽，最近怎么样？

李丽：还不错！你呢？

杰明：非常好，也非常开心！因为我妈妈会来看我。

李丽：太好了！她什么时候到？

杰明：她下星期五早上到，我和苏飞会去飞机场接她。

李丽：你爸爸呢？也会一起来吗？

杰明：不会，我爸爸的工作很忙，来不了。

李丽：对了，你有兄弟姐妹吗？

杰明：我有一个姐姐和两个哥哥。你呢？

李丽：我有一个弟弟，在上学。

杰明：他多大？

李丽：17岁了。你看，这是他的照片！

杰明：嗯，你弟弟看上去很帅！

李丽：你的姐姐和哥哥呢？

杰明：他们都工作了。我的姐姐是律师，两个哥哥都是电脑工程师。

李丽：真酷！对了，你妈妈今年多大？

杰明：我妈妈今年53岁。

李丽：她以前来过中国吗？

杰明：没有。这是第一次！所以她非常激动！

李丽：太好了！祝你们玩得开心！

杰明：谢谢你！

6 去 沃 尔 玛 购 物
qù wò ěr mǎ gòu wù

SHOPPING IN WALMART

sū fēi nǐ kàn qiánmiàn jiù shì wò ěr mǎ chāo shì
苏飞：你看，前面就是**沃尔玛超市**。
Su Fei: Look, **Walmart** is right ahead.

jié míng wā zhè gè chāo shì zhēn dà
杰明：哇！这个**超市**真大。
Jamie: Wow! This **supermarket** is really big.

sū fēi dāng rán hěn duō rén dōu xǐ huān zài wò ěr mǎ mǎi dōng xī hěn fāng biàn
苏飞：当然！很多人都喜欢在沃尔玛**买东西**，很**方便**、
xuǎn zé yě duō
选择也多。
Su Fei: Of course! Many people like to **buy things** at Walmart, it's very **convenient** and has a wide range of **choices**.

jié míng kàn lái wò ěr mǎ hěn yǒu míng
杰明：看来，沃尔玛很**有名**！
Jamie: It looks like Walmart is very **famous**!

sū fēi ng zhè lǐ de dōng xī yě bù cuò wǒ měi gè zhōu mò dōu huì lái zhè
苏飞：嗯！这里的东西也**不错**，我每个**周末**都会来这
lǐ mǎi cài
里**买菜**。
Su Fei: Well! Things here are also **good**, I come here every **weekend** to **buy groceries**.

jié míng jīn tiān rén hěn duō hǎo xiàng yǒu diǎn ér jǐ
杰明：今天人很多，好像有点儿**挤**！

Jamie: So many people here today, looks a bit **crowded**!

sū fēi　shì ā　zhōu mò mǎi cài dōu jǐ
苏飞:是啊！周末**买菜**都挤。
Su Fei: Indeed! **Grocery shopping** on weekends is always like this.

jié míng　wǒ yào mǎi hěn duō dōng xī　shū cài　shuǐ guǒ hé ròu
杰明:我**要**买很多东西—**蔬菜**，水果和肉。
Jamie: **I want to** buy a lot of things - **vegetables**, fruits, and meat.

sū fēi　zhè lǐ yǒu xiāng jiāo　píng guǒ　jú zǐ hé pú táo
苏飞:这里有香蕉、苹果、橘子和葡萄。
Su Fei: **Here** are bananas, apples, oranges, and grapes.

jié míng　duì le　xiāng jiāo hé pú táo duō shǎo qián yī jīn
杰明:对了，香蕉和葡萄**多少钱**一斤？
Jamie: By the way, **how much** are bananas and grapes per catty?

sū fēi　wǒ kàn yī kàn　xiāng jiāo　kuài qián yī jīn　pú táo　kuài qián yī jīn
苏飞:我**看一看**，香蕉5块钱**一斤**，葡萄18块钱一斤。
Su Fei: Let me **take a look**. Bananas are 5 Yuan **per catty** and grapes are 18 Yuan per catty.

jié míng kàn lái　xiāng jiāo hěn pián yi　pú táo yǒu diǎn ér guì
杰明:看来，香蕉很**便宜**，葡萄有点儿**贵**。
Jamie: It seems bananas are very **cheap**, and grapes are a bit **expensive**.

sū fēi　nǐ yào mǎi nǎ xiē shū cài
苏飞:你要买**哪些**蔬菜？
Su Fei: **Which** vegetables do you want to buy?

jié míng　wǒ yào mǎi bái cài　tǔ dòu　xī hóng shì hé xī lán huā
杰明:我要买**白菜**、土豆、西红柿和**西兰花**。
Jamie: I want to buy **cabbage**, potatoes, tomatoes, and **broccoli**.

sū fēi　hái yǒu ma
苏飞:还有吗？
Su Fei: Anything else?

jié míng　hái yǒu miàn bāo　zhū ròu　niú ròu　jī dàn hé yú
杰明:还有面包、猪肉、牛肉、鸡蛋和鱼。
Jamie: **Also**, bread, pork, beef, eggs, and fish.

sū fēi　dōng xī dōu zài qián miàn　wǒ men guò qù ba
苏飞:东西都在**前面**，我们**过去**吧。
Su Fei: Everything is **ahead**, let's **go over**.

shí fēn zhōng hòu
十分钟后…
10 minutes later...

杰明： <ruby>都<rt>dōu</rt></ruby> <ruby>买<rt>mǎi</rt></ruby> <ruby>好<rt>hǎo</rt></ruby> <ruby>了<rt>le</rt></ruby>！
jié míng

Jamie: I bought it all!

苏飞： <ruby>这<rt>zhè</rt></ruby> <ruby>是<rt>shì</rt></ruby> **<ruby>自<rt>zì</rt></ruby> <ruby>助<rt>zhù</rt></ruby> <ruby>付<rt>fù</rt></ruby> <ruby>款<rt>kuǎn</rt></ruby> <ruby>机<rt>jī</rt></ruby>**，<ruby>你<rt>nǐ</rt></ruby> <ruby>可<rt>kě</rt></ruby> <ruby>以<rt>yǐ</rt></ruby> **<ruby>用<rt>yòng</rt></ruby>** <ruby>手<rt>shǒu</rt></ruby> <ruby>机<rt>jī</rt></ruby> **<ruby>扫<rt>sǎo</rt></ruby> <ruby>码<rt>mǎ</rt></ruby>** <ruby>付<rt>fù</rt></ruby> <ruby>款<rt>kuǎn</rt></ruby>。
sū fēi

Su Fei: This is a **self-check-out machine**. You can **use** mobile phone to **scan the QR code** to pay.

杰明： <ruby>好<rt>hǎo</rt></ruby> <ruby>的<rt>de</rt></ruby>。**<ruby>一<rt>yī</rt></ruby> <ruby>共<rt>gòng</rt></ruby> <ruby>才<rt>cái</rt></ruby>** 120 <ruby>块<rt>kuài</rt></ruby> <ruby>钱<rt>qián</rt></ruby>，**<ruby>不<rt>bù</rt></ruby> <ruby>贵<rt>guì</rt></ruby>**！
jié míng

Jamie: Okay. **A total of** only 120 Yuan, not **expensive**!

苏飞： <ruby>是<rt>shì</rt></ruby> <ruby>啊<rt>ā</rt></ruby>，<ruby>比<rt>bǐ</rt></ruby> <ruby>英<rt>yīng</rt></ruby> <ruby>国<rt>guó</rt></ruby> <ruby>的<rt>de</rt></ruby> **<ruby>便<rt>pián</rt></ruby> <ruby>宜<rt>yi</rt></ruby> <ruby>多<rt>duō</rt></ruby> <ruby>了<rt>le</rt></ruby>**！
sū fēi

Su Fei: Indeed, **much cheaper** than the UK!

杰明： <ruby>嗯<rt>ng</rt></ruby>，<ruby>谢<rt>xiè</rt></ruby> <ruby>谢<rt>xie</rt></ruby> <ruby>你<rt>nǐ</rt></ruby> **<ruby>帮<rt>bāng</rt></ruby> <ruby>我<rt>wǒ</rt></ruby>**！
jié míng

Jamie: True, thank you for **helping** me!

苏飞： <ruby>不<rt>bù</rt></ruby> <ruby>客<rt>kè</rt></ruby> <ruby>气<rt>qì</rt></ruby>！
sū fēi

Su Fei: You're welcome!

Learning Tip

斤 (jīn) is a standard measurement of weight in China. It is sometimes translated to English as "catty" and is equivalent to 600g or approximately 21 ounces.

Culture Corner

In recent years it has become far less common for people to use cash in China. Whether in markets, shops, or even vending machines, people tend to use mobile apps such as WeChat to make payments often by scanning a QR code.

Key Vocabulary

wò ěr mǎ 沃尔玛	*n.*	Walmart	chāo shì 超市	*n.*	supermarket
fāng biàn 方便	*adj.*	convenient	xuǎn zé 选择	*v.*	to choose
kàn lái 看来	*adv.*	seem	zhōu mò 周末	*n.*	weekend
mǎi cài 买菜	*vp.*	to buy groceries	jǐ 挤	*adj.*	crowded
shū cài 蔬菜	*n.*	vegetables	duō shǎo qián 多少钱		how much
pián yi 便宜	*adj.*	cheap	guì 贵	*adj.*	expensive
zì zhù fù kuǎn jī 自助付款机	*n.*	self-checkout machine	cái 才	*adv.*	only
sǎo mǎ 扫码	*vp.*	to scan a code (e.g. QR, barcode)	bāng 帮	*v.*	to help

Chinese Version

苏 飞：你看，前面就是沃尔玛超市。

杰 明：哇！这个超市真大。

苏 飞：当然！很多人都喜欢在沃尔玛买东西，很方便、选择也多。

杰 明：看来，沃尔玛很有名！

苏 飞：嗯！这里的东西也不错，我每个周末都会来这里买菜。

杰 明：今天人很多，好像有点儿挤！

苏 飞：是啊！周末买菜都挤。

杰 明：我要买很多东西—蔬菜，水果和肉。

苏 飞：这里有香蕉、苹果、橘子和葡萄。

杰 明：对了，香蕉和葡萄多少钱一斤？

苏 飞：我看一看，香蕉5块钱一斤，葡萄18块钱一斤。

杰 明：看来，香蕉很便宜，葡萄有点儿贵。

苏 飞：你要买哪些蔬菜？

杰 明：我要买白菜、土豆、西红柿和西兰花。

苏 飞：还有吗？

杰 明：还有面包、猪肉、牛肉、鸡蛋和鱼。

苏 飞：东西都在前面，我们过去吧。

10分钟后⋯

杰 明：都买好了！

苏 飞：这是自助付款机，你可以用手机扫码付款。

杰 明：好的。一共才120块钱，不贵！

苏 飞：是啊，比英国的便宜多了！

杰 明：嗯，谢谢你帮我！

苏 飞：不客气！

7

去 饭 馆
qù　fàn　guǎn

GOING TO THE RESTAURANT

sū fēi　jiù shì zhè jiā fàn guǎn　wǒ men jìn qù ba
苏飞：就是这家**饭馆**，我们进去吧。
Su Fei: This is the **restaurant**, let's go in.

jié míng　hǎo　ā
杰明：好啊！
Jamie: Okay!

fú wù yuán　huān yíng　qǐng wèn jǐ wèi
服务员：欢迎，请问几位？
Waitress: **Welcome**, how many of you?

sū fēi　jiù wǒ men liǎng gè rén
苏飞：就我们两个人。
Su Fei: **Just** the two of us.

fú wù yuán　hǎo de　qǐng jìn　liǎng wèi qǐng zuò　zhè shì cài dān
服务员：好的，**请进**！两位**请坐**！这是**菜单**。
Waitress: Okay, **come in**! Please **take a seat**. This is the **menu**.

jié míng　xiè xie　wǒ kàn yī kàn　wǒ yào yī pán běi jīng kǎo yā hé yī wǎn chǎo fàn
杰明：谢谢！我**看一看**。我要一盘**北京烤鸭**和一碗**炒饭**。
Jamie: Thank you! Let me **take a look**. I want a plate of **Peking duck** and a
bowl of **fried rice**.

sū fēi　wǒ yào yī fèn gōng bào jī dīng hé yī fèn xī hóng shì chǎo jī dàn
苏飞：我要一份宫爆鸡丁和一份西红柿炒鸡蛋。
Su Fei: I want a portion of **Gong Bao Chicken** and a portion of **Scrambled Eggs with Tomatoes.**

shí fēn zhōng hòu
十分钟后......
10 minutes later......

fú wù yuán　hǎo de　qǐng wèn nǐ men yào hē shén me ma
服务员：好的！请问你们要喝什么吗？
Waitress: Okay! What would you like to **drink**?

jié míng　wǒ yào yī bēi lǜ chá
杰明：我要一杯绿茶。
Jamie: I want a cup of **green tea.**

sū fēi　wǒ yào yī píng kě lè
苏飞：我要一瓶可乐。
Su Fei: I want a bottle of **cola.**

fú wù yuán　hǎo de　qǐng shāo děng
服务员：好的！请稍等。
Waitress: OK! Please **wait a moment.**

fú wù yuán　zhè shì nǐ men de cài　qǐng màn yòng
服务员：这是你们的菜，请慢用！
Waitress: Here are your dishes, **please enjoy** (use slowly)!

sū fēi　hǎo de　xiè xie
苏飞：好的，谢谢！
Su Fei: OK, thank you!

jié míng　ā　zhè xiē cài kàn shàng qù zhēn bù cuò　wǒ yào quán bù chī wán
杰明：啊！这些菜看上去真不错，我要全部吃完！
Jamie: Ah! **These** dishes look **so good**, I want to eat them **all**!

sū fēi　nǐ zhēn shì gè chī huò
苏飞：你真是个吃货！
Su Fei: You are such a **foodie!**

jié míng　duì　wǒ jiù shì gè dà chī huò
杰明：对，我就是个大吃货！
Jamie: Yes, I am a super foodie!

sū fēi　zhè yǒu yī shuāng kuài zǐ　nǐ huì yòng ma
苏飞：这有一双筷子，你会用吗？
Su Fei: Here are **a pair of chopsticks**, can you **use** them?

jié míng bù huì   dàn shì wǒ yào shì yī shì   xiàn zài zài zhōng guó   wǒ yī dìng yào
杰明：不会，但是我要**试一试**。现在在中国，我**一定**要
xué huì yòng kuài zǐ
学会用**筷子**。

Jamie: No, but I want to **try** it. Now I am in China, **I must** learn to use **chopsticks**.

sān shí fēn zhōng hòu
三十分钟后...

After 30 minutes...

jié míng zhēn hǎo chī   fú wù yuán wǒ yào mǎi dān
杰明：真好吃！服务员，我要**买单**。

Jamie: It's so **delicious**! Waitress, I want to **pay the bill**.

fú wù yuán xiān shēng yī gòng   kuài qián
服务员：先生，**一共**80**块钱**！

Waitress: Sir, in total 80 Yuan, please!

jié míng ng   wǒ yòng wēi xìn fù ba
杰明：嗯，我**用微信付**吧。

Jamie: OK, I will **pay by WeChat**.

fú wù yuán kě yǐ   qǐng zài zhè lǐ sǎo mǎ
服务员：可以，请在这里**扫码**！

Waitress: Of course, please **scan the code** here!

jié míng hǎo de
杰明：好的。

Jamie: All right.

fú wù yuán xiè xie   huān yíng xià cì zài lái
服务员：谢谢！欢迎**下次**再来。

Waitress: Thank you! See you **next time**.

Learning Tip

chī huò
吃货 literally means "eating goods" it is a slang term meaning "foodie" and as you might expect it is used to describe someone who loves eating a lot.

Key Vocabulary

fàn guǎn 饭馆	*n.*	restaurant	huānyíng 欢迎	*v.*	welcome
cài dān 菜单	*n.*	menu	lǜ chá 绿茶	*n.*	green tea
kě lè 可乐	*n.*	cola	cài 菜	*n.*	dish
bù cuò 不错	*adj.*	very good	quán bù 全部	*adj.*	all
yī shuāng 一双		a pair of	kuài zǐ 筷子	*n.*	chopsticks
dàn shì 但是	*conj.*	but	xiàn zài 现在	*n.*	now
yī dìng 一定	*adv.*	must	hǎo chī 好吃	*adj.*	delicious
mǎi dān 买单	*v.*	to pay the bill	yī gòng 一共	*adv.*	in total

Chinese Version

苏飞：就是这家饭馆，我们进去吧。

杰明：好啊！

服务员：欢迎，请问几位？

苏飞：就我们两个人。

服务员：好的，请进！两位请坐！这是菜单。

杰明：谢谢！我看一看。我要一盘北京烤鸭和一碗炒饭。

苏飞：我要一份宫爆鸡丁和一份西红柿炒鸡蛋。

服务员：好的！请问你们要喝什么吗？

杰明：我要一杯绿茶。

苏飞：我要一瓶可乐。

服务员：好的！请稍等。

10分钟后...

服务员：这是你们的菜，请慢用！

苏飞：好的，谢谢！

杰明：啊！这些菜看上去真不错，我要全部吃完！

苏飞：你真是个吃货！

杰明：对，我就是个大吃货！

苏飞：这有一双筷子，你会用吗？

杰明：不会，但是我要试一试。现在在中国，我一定要学会用筷子。

30分钟后...

杰明：真好吃！服务员，我要买单。

服务员：先生，一共80块钱！

杰明：嗯，我用微信付吧。

服务员：可以，请在这里扫码！

杰明：好的。

服务员：谢谢！欢迎下次再来。

8 点外卖
diǎn wài mài

ORDERING A TAKEAWAY

sū fēi wǒ jué dé hǎo è kě shì bù xiǎng zuò fàn
苏飞:我觉得好**饿**！可是不想**做饭**。
Su Fei: I feel so **hungry**! But I don't want to **cook**.

jié míng wǒ yě shì gǎn jué jīn tiān tè bié lǎn
杰明:我也是，**感觉**今天**特别懒**！
Jamie: Me too, I **feel** especially **lazy** today!

sū fēi yào bù wǒ men diǎn wài mài ba
苏飞:要不，我们点**外卖**吧！
Su Fei: Maybe, let's order **takeaway**!

jié míng hǎo zhǔ yì
杰明:好主意！
Jamie: Good idea!

sū fēi nǐ zhī dào zěn me diǎn wài mài ma
苏飞:你知道**怎么**点外卖吗？
Su Fei: Do you know **how to** order takeaway?

jié míng hái bù zhī dào nǐ gào sù wǒ zěn me diǎn ba
杰明:还不知道，你**告诉**我怎么点吧。
Jamie: Not yet. **Tell** me how to do it.

sū fēi nǐ yòng shǒu jī jiù kě yǐ diǎn xià zǎi wài mài de shǒu jī chéng xù měi
苏飞:你用**手机**就可以点。**下载**外卖的手机**程序**"美
tuán wài mài zài shàng miàn diǎn
团外卖"，在上面点。

Su Fei: You can order with your **mobile**. **Download** the takeaway mobile **app** "Meituan Waimai" to order it.

<small>jié míng hǎo de wǒ xiàn zài jiù xià zǎi</small>
杰明：好的，我**现在**就**下载**！

Jamie: Okay, I will download it **now**!

<small>sū fēi   měi tuán shàng yǒu hěn duō fàn guǎn kě yǐ xuǎn zé   yě yǒu hěn duō yòu hǎo</small>
苏飞："**美团**"上有很多**饭馆**可以**选择**，也有很多又**好**
<small>chī yòu pián yi de fàn cài</small>
吃又便宜的**饭菜**。

Su Fei: There are many **restaurants** on "Meituan" **to choose from**, and there are also many **delicious** and cheap **dishes**.

<small>jié míng jiù shì shuō   wǒ xiǎng chī shén me   jiù diǎn shén me ma</small>
杰明：就是说，我想吃什么，就**点什么**吗？

Jamie: **So you're saying** that I can **order whatever** I want to eat?

<small>sū fēi   duì   diǎn wán hòu   jiù huì yǒu sòng cān rén yuán bǎ fàn cài sòng dào nǐ jiā</small>
苏飞：对！点完**后**，就会有**送餐人员**把饭菜送到你**家**。

Su Fei: Yes! **After** ordering, a **delivery person** will deliver the food to your **home**.

<small>jié míng tài bàng le   wǒ xiàn zài jiù diǎn yī wǎn miàn hé yī píng kě lè</small>
杰明：太棒了！我现在就点**一碗面**和**一瓶可乐**。

Jamie: That's great! I will order **a bowl of noodles** and **a bottle of coke** now.

<small>sū fēi   wǒ yě lái diǎn</small>
苏飞：我也来点。

Su Fei: Let me order it too.

<small>jié míng nǐ diǎn le shén me</small>
杰明：你点了什么？

Jamie: What did you order?

<small>sū fēi   wǒ diǎn le yī wǎn niú ròu fàn hé yī bēi suān nǎi</small>
苏飞：我点了**一碗牛肉饭**和**一杯酸奶**。

Su Fei: **A bowl of beef rice** and **a cup of yogurt**.

<small>jié míng hǎo le   nà xiàn zài wǒ men jiù děng sòng cān rén yuán ba   duì le   huì</small>
杰明：好了！那现在我们就**等送餐人员**吧！**对了**，会
<small>děng duō jiǔ</small>
等多久？

Jamie: Alright! Then let's wait for the **delivery person** now. **By the way**, how long do we have to wait?

<small>sū fēi   fàng xīn   chà bù duō   fēn zhōng jiù huì sòng dào</small>
苏飞：放心！**差不多**20**分钟**就会送到。

Su Fei: Don't worry! It'll be **about** 20 **minutes**.

jié míng　tài hǎo le　zhè gè chéng xù zhēn fāng biàn
杰明：太好了！这个 程 序真方便！
Jamie: That's great! This **app** is so **convenient**!

sū fēi　dāng rán　xiàn zài dà jiā dōu yòng
苏飞：当然！现在大家都用。
Su Fei: Of course! **Everyone** is using it now.

jié míng　duì le　nǐ jīng cháng diǎn wài mài ma
杰明：对了，你经常点外卖吗？
Jamie: By the way, do you **often** order takeaways?

sū fēi　bù jīng cháng　měi liǎng xīng qī yī cì
苏飞：不经常，每两星期一次。
Su Fei: Not often, **once** every two weeks.

Culture Corner

měi tuán wài mài
美 团 外 卖 is a popular app for ordering takeaway food in China. Not only can you order food but you also order other commodities for fast delivery

37

Key Vocabulary

è 饿	*adj.*	hungry		lǎn 懒	*adj.*	lazy	
diǎn 点	*v.*	to order		wài mài 外卖	*n.*	takeaway	
zěn me 怎么	*pro.*	how		gào sù 告诉	*v.*	tell	
shǒu jī 手机	*n.*	mobile		chéng xù 程序	*n.*	app	
sòng cān rén yuán 送餐人员	*n.*	food delivery staff		yī wǎn 一碗		a bowl of	
suān nǎi 酸奶	*n.*	yogurt		duō jiǔ 多久		how long?	
chà bù duō 差不多	*adv.*	about		dà jiā 大家	*pro.*	everyone	

Chinese Version

苏飞：我觉得好饿！可是不想做饭。

杰明：我也是，感觉今天特别懒！

苏飞：要不，我们点外卖吧！

杰明：好主意！

苏飞：你知道怎么点外卖吗？

杰明：还不知道，你告诉我怎么点吧。

苏飞：你用手机就可以点。下载外卖的手机程序"美团外卖"，在上面
点。

杰明：好的，我现在就下载！

苏飞：美团上有很多饭馆可以选择，也有很多又好吃又便宜的饭菜。

杰明：就是说，我想吃什么，就点什么吗？

苏飞：对！点完后，就会有送餐人员把饭菜送到你家。

杰明：太棒了！我现在就点一碗面和一瓶可乐。

苏飞：我也来点。

杰明：你点了什么？

苏飞：我点了一碗牛肉饭和一杯酸奶。

杰明：好了！那现在我们就等送餐人员吧！对了，会等多久？

苏飞：放心！差不多20分钟就会送到。

杰明：太好了！这个程序真方便！

苏飞：当然！现在大家都用。

杰明：对了，你经常点外卖吗？

苏飞：不经常，每两星期一次。

9 坐 地 铁 去 机 场
zuò dì tiě qù jī chǎng
TAKING METRO TO THE AIRPORT

sū fēi　jié míng　nǐ zhǔn bèi hǎo le ma
苏飞：杰明，你**准备好**了吗？
Su Fei: Jamie, are you **ready** (well prepared)?

jié míng zhǔn bèi hǎo le　　wǒ men zǒu ba
杰明：准备好了，**我们走吧**。
Jamie: Yes, **let's go**.

sū fēi　xiàn zài　jǐ diǎn le
苏飞：现在**几点**了？
Su Fei: What's the time now?

jié míng　jiǔ diǎn　wǒ mā mā shì shí diǎn de fēi jī
杰明：九点，我妈妈是十点的**飞机**。
Jamie: Nine o'clock, my mum's **plane** will arrive at ten o'clock.

sū fēi　hái yǒu yī gè xiǎo shí　bù yòng zháo jí
苏飞：**还有**一个小时，不用**着急**。
Su Fei: Still one hour left, don't **worry**.

jié míng　duì le　　nǐ xiǎng zuò chū zū chē　hái shì zuò dì tiě
杰明：对了，你想**坐出租车**，还是**坐地铁**？
Jamie: By the way, do you want to **take a taxi** or **take the metro**?

sū fēi　chū zū chē yǒu diǎn guì　wǒ men zuò dì tiě ba
苏飞：出租车**有点**贵，我们坐地铁吧。
Su Fei: Taxis are **a bit** expensive. Let's take the metro.

杰明：可以！**而且**，坐地铁也一样**快**。等我们**接**到妈妈，再坐出租车**回来**。

Jamie: OK! **Besides**, taking the metro is just as **fast**. When we **pick up** my mum, we can take a taxi **back**.

苏飞：我**同意**，那我们现在就去**地铁站**吧。

Su Fei: I **agree**, let's go to the **metro station** now.

五分钟后…

5 minutes later…

苏飞：你看，这是**自助售票机**，你可以在这里**买票**。

Su Fei: Look, this is a **self-service ticket machine**. You can **buy tickets** here.

杰明：哇！语言有**中文**的，也有**英文**的。

Jamie: Wow! It has **Chinese** and **English**.

苏飞：我们**用**中文的吧。

Su Fei: Let's **use** Chinese.

杰明：好的。**我看看**，一共四个**站**，30分钟就能**到**飞机场！

Jamie: Okay. **Let me see**, there are four **stations** in total and it'll take 30 minutes to **arrive at** the airport!

苏飞：你**只用**买你自己的票。我有**地铁卡，不用**买票。

Su Fei: You **only** need to buy your own ticket. I have a **metro card**, so I **don't need to** buy tickets.

杰明：好的！

Jamie: Okay!

苏飞：我们**上车**吧。**现在**人不多，有很多**座位**。

Su Fei: Let's **get in**. There are not many people **now**, lots of **seats** available.

杰明：我很喜欢中国的地铁，很**新**、也很**舒服**。

41

Jamie: I like the metro in China a lot. It's very **new** and **comfortable**.

<ruby>苏<rt>sū</rt></ruby><ruby>飞<rt>fēi</rt></ruby>：<ruby>当<rt>dāng</rt></ruby><ruby>然<rt>rán</rt></ruby><ruby>了<rt>le</rt></ruby>！<ruby>现<rt>xiàn</rt></ruby><ruby>在<rt>zài</rt></ruby><ruby>中<rt>zhōng</rt></ruby><ruby>国<rt>guó</rt></ruby><ruby>的<rt>de</rt></ruby><ruby>大<rt>dà</rt></ruby><ruby>城<rt>chéng</rt></ruby><ruby>市<rt>shì</rt></ruby><ruby>都<rt>dōu</rt></ruby><ruby>有<rt>yǒu</rt></ruby><ruby>地<rt>dì</rt></ruby><ruby>铁<rt>tiě</rt></ruby>，<ruby>出<rt>chū</rt></ruby><ruby>门<rt>mén</rt></ruby><ruby>很<rt>hěn</rt></ruby><ruby>方<rt>fāng</rt></ruby><ruby>便<rt>biàn</rt></ruby>。

Su Fei: Of course! **Nowadays** there are metros in all **major cities** in China, making it easy to **go out**.

<ruby>三<rt>sān</rt></ruby><ruby>十<rt>shí</rt></ruby><ruby>分<rt>fēn</rt></ruby><ruby>钟<rt>zhōng</rt></ruby><ruby>后<rt>hòu</rt></ruby>…

After 30 minutes…

<ruby>苏<rt>sū</rt></ruby><ruby>飞<rt>fēi</rt></ruby>：<ruby>飞<rt>fēi</rt></ruby><ruby>机<rt>jī</rt></ruby><ruby>场<rt>chǎng</rt></ruby><ruby>到<rt>dào</rt></ruby><ruby>了<rt>le</rt></ruby>，<ruby>我<rt>wǒ</rt></ruby><ruby>们<rt>men</rt></ruby><ruby>下<rt>xià</rt></ruby><ruby>车<rt>chē</rt></ruby><ruby>吧<rt>ba</rt></ruby>.

Su Fei: Here is the **airport**, let's **get off**.

<ruby>杰<rt>jié</rt></ruby><ruby>明<rt>míng</rt></ruby>：<ruby>真<rt>zhēn</rt></ruby><ruby>是<rt>shì</rt></ruby><ruby>太<rt>tài</rt></ruby><ruby>快<rt>kuài</rt></ruby><ruby>了<rt>le</rt></ruby>！

Jamie: So fast!

Key Vocabulary

zhǔn bèi 准 备	*v.*	to prepare		jǐ diǎn 几 点		what time
fēi jī 飞 机	*n.*	airplane		zháo jí 着 急	*adj.*	anxious / worried
chū zū chē 出 租 车	*n.*	taxi		dì tiě 地 铁	*n.*	metro
ér qiě 而 且	*conj.*	besides		jiē 接	*v.*	to pick up
tóng yì 同 意	*v.*	to agree		dì tiě zhàn 地 铁 站	*n.*	metro station
fēi jī chǎng 飞 机 场	*n.*	airport		piào 票	*n.*	ticket
shàng chē 上 车	*v.*	to get in a vehicle		xià chē 下 车	*v.*	to get off
xīn 新	*adj.*	new		shū fú 舒 服	*adj.*	comfortable
zuò wèi 座 位	*n.*	seat		chū mén 出 门	*vp.*	to go out

43

Chinese Version

苏飞：杰明，你准备好了吗？

杰明：准备好了，我们走吧。

苏飞：现在几点了？

杰明：九点，我妈妈是十点的飞机。

苏飞：还有一个小时，不用着急。

杰明：对了，你想坐出租车，还是坐地铁？

苏飞：出租车有点贵，我们坐地铁吧。

杰明：可以！而且，坐地铁也一样快。等我们接到妈妈，再坐出租车回来。

苏飞：我同意，那我们现在就去地铁站吧。

5 分钟后…

苏飞：你看，这是自助售票机，你可以在这里买票。

杰明：哇！语言有中文的，也有英文的。

苏飞：我们用中文的吧。

杰明：好的。我看看，一共四个站，30 分钟就能到飞机场！

苏飞：你只用买你自己的票。我有地铁卡，不用买票。

杰明：好的！

苏飞：我们上车吧。现在人不多，有很多座位。

杰明：我很喜欢中国的地铁，很新、也很舒服。

苏飞：当然了！现在中国的大城市都有地铁，出门很方便。

30 分钟后…

苏飞：飞机场到了，我们下车吧.

杰明：真是太快了！

10 你 喜 欢 做 什 么?

nǐ xǐ huān zuò shén me

WHAT DO YOU LIKE TO DO?

李丽：在**周末**，你喜欢做什么？
lǐ lì zài zhōu mò nǐ xǐ huān zuò shén me

Li Li: What do you like to do on **weekends**?

杰明：我喜欢看**电影**，特别是**科幻**电影，你呢？
jié míng wǒ xǐ huān kàn diàn yǐng tè bié shì kē huàn diàn yǐng nǐ ne

Jamie: I like watching **movies**, especially **science fiction** movies. What about you?

李丽：我喜欢看**小说**，也喜欢和朋友们**骑自行车**到处玩。
lǐ lì wǒ xǐ huān kàn xiǎo shuō yě xǐ huān hé péng yǒu men qí zì xíng chē dào chù wán

Li Li: I like reading **novels**, and like to **ride bicycles** around with my friends.

杰明：那你有自己的**自行车**吗？
jié míng nà nǐ yǒu zì jǐ de zì xíng chē ma

Jamie: Do you have your own **bicycle**?

李丽：没有。**现在**在中国，大家都**不用**买自行车了，都用"共享单车"。
lǐ lì méi yǒu xiàn zài zài zhōng guó dà jiā dōu bù yòng mǎi zì xíng chē le dōu yòng gòngxiǎng dān chē

Li Li: No. **Now** in China, people **don't need to** buy bicycles, they **all** use "shared bicycles".

杰明：你说的"共享单车"，是**街上**那些**彩色**的自行
车吗？

Jamie: Are the "shared bicycles" those **colourful** bicycles **on the street**?

李丽：对！这些自行车非常**方便**，用**手机扫码**就可
以骑。

Li Li: Yes! These bicycles are very **convenient** and you can ride them by
scanning the code with mobile phone.

杰明：贵吗？

Jamie: Is it expensive?

李丽：不贵！我**每个月**才花10块钱，想什么时候骑，
就什么时候骑。

Li Li: No! I only **spend** 10 Yuan **per month**, and I can **ride** whenever I want.

杰明：在**城市**里，**到处**都有这些自行车吗？

Jamie: Are these bicycles **everywhere** in the **city**?

李丽：对！**所以**，你想骑到哪里都可以。

Li Li: Yes! **That's why** you can ride wherever you want.

杰明：那**停车**呢？

Jamie: What about **parking**?

李丽：**任何**有"共享单车"的**地方**，都可以**停车**。

Li Li: **Any place** that has "shared bicycles", you can all **park**.

杰明：这**听上去**太方便了！

Jamie: This **sounds** so convenient!

李丽：是啊！**以前**大家**得**买自行车，现在不用了。

Li Li: Yes! **In the past**, everyone **had to** buy bicycles, but now there is no need.

杰明：的确！**而且**，买的车子也容易**被偷**！

Jamie: Indeed! **Besides**, privately-owned bicycles are also easily **stolen**!

李丽：你的**自行车**被偷过吗？
lǐ lì nǐ de zì xíng chē bèi tōu guò ma

Li Li: Did your **bicycle** get stolen before?

杰明：当然！在**伦敦**的时候，被偷过**两次**。
jié míng dāng rán zài lún dūn de shí hòu bèi tōu guò liǎng cì

Jamie: Of course! In **London**, it was stolen **twice**.

李丽：真**倒霉**！
lǐ lì zhēn dǎo méi

Li Li: What **bad luck**!

杰明：**不过**，现在不用**担心**了！
jié míng bù guo xiàn zài bù yòng dān xīn le

Jamie: **However**, now I don't need to **worry** anymore!

李丽：嗯，你可以**下载**"**共享单车**"的**手机程序**，这样更**方便**。
lǐ lì ng nǐ kě yǐ xià zǎi gòngxiǎng dān chē de shǒu jī chéng xù zhè yàng gèng fāng biàn

Li Li: Well, you can **download** the "bicycle-sharing" **mobile app**, more **convenient**.

杰明：我现在就去下载，**一会儿**骑自行车**回**学校。
jié míng wǒ xiàn zài jiù qù xià zǎi yī huì ér qí zì xíng chē huí xué xiào

Jamie: I will download it now and ride the bicycle **back to** campus **later**.

Culture Corner

共享单车
gòng xiǎng dān chē

共享单车 (bicycle sharing) is a popular service in big cities in China. You can find bikes on almost every major street, which can be unlocked and used simply by scanning with an app on your phone.

Key Vocabulary

diàn yǐng
电 影   *n.*   film

kē huàn
科 幻   *n.*   science fiction

xiǎo shuō
小 说   *n.*   novel

qí
骑   *v.*   to ride

zì xíng chē
自 行 车   *n.*   bike

bù yòng
不 用   *adv.*   no need

cǎi sè
彩 色   *adj.*   colourful

měi
每   *pro.*   every (day, hour, etc...)

chéng shì
城 市   *n.*   city

tíng chē
停 车   *v.*   to park

yǐ qián
以 前   *n.*   in the past

dí què
的 确   *adv.*   indeed

tōu
偷   *v.*   to steal

dǎo méi
倒 霉   *adj.*   bad luck

dān xīn
担 心   *adj.* worry / *v.* to worry

yī huì ér
一 会 儿   *n.*   later

Chinese Version

李丽：在周末，你喜欢做什么？

杰明：我喜欢看电影，特别是科幻电影，你呢？

李丽：我喜欢看小说，也喜欢和朋友们骑自行车到处玩。

杰明：那你有自己的自行车吗？

李丽：没有。现在在中国，大家都不用买自行车了，都用"共享单车"。

杰明：你说的"共享单车"，是街上那些彩色的自行车吗？

李丽：对！这些自行车非常方便，用手机扫码就可以骑。

杰明：贵吗？

李丽：不贵！我每个月才花10块钱，想什么时候骑，就什么时候骑。

杰明：在城市里，到处都有这些自行车吗？

李丽：对！所以，你想骑到哪里都可以。

杰明：那停车呢？

李丽：任何有"共享单车"的地方，都可以停车。

杰明：这听上去太方便了！

李丽：是啊！以前大家得买自行车，现在不用了。

杰明：的确！而且，买的车子也容易被偷！

李丽：你的自行车被偷过吗？

杰明：当然！在伦敦的时候，被偷过两次。

李丽：真倒霉！

杰明：不过，现在不用担心了！

李丽：嗯，你可以下载"共享单车"的手机程序，这样更方便。

杰明：我现在就去下载，一会儿骑自行车回学校。

11 　我的中文名字
wǒ de zhōng wén míng zì

MY CHINESE NAME

lǐ lì　nǐ hé sū fēi shì shén me shí hòu rèn shí de
李丽：你和苏飞是什么时候认识的？
Li Li:　**When** did you and Su Fei meet?

jié míng　shì qù nián liù yuè fèn rèn shí de
杰明：是去年六月份认识的。
Jamie:　We met in June **last year**.

lǐ lì　wǒ jué dé nǐ hěn xǐ huān tā
李丽：我觉得你很喜欢她。
Li Li:　I **think** you like her very much.

jié míng dāng rán le　　tā shì wǒ zài zhōng guó zuì hǎo de péng yǒu
杰明：当然了！她是我在中国最好的朋友。
Jamie:　Of course! She is my **best friend** in China.

lǐ lì　xiàn zài wǒ hé tā yě shì péng yǒu le　hái jīng cháng yī qǐ chī fàn
李丽：现在我和她也是朋友了，还经常一起吃饭。
Li Li:　Now, she and I are friends **too**, we often eat **together**.

jié míng　shì ma　zhè tài bàng le
杰明：是吗？这太棒了！
Jamie:　Really? That's **great**!

lǐ lì　wǒ jué dé nǐ de zhōng wén míng zì hěn tè bié
李丽：我觉得你的中文名字很特别！
Li Li:　I **think** your Chinese name is very **unique**!

杰明：**其实**，这个中文名字也是苏飞**帮我取**的。

Jamie: **Actually**, it was also Su Fei who **helped me pick** this Chinese name.

李丽：**那么**，这个名字是什么**意思**呢？

Li Li: **So**, what's the **meaning** of the name?

杰明："杰"是"**杰出**"的"杰"，"明"是"**聪明**"的"明"。

Jamie: "Jié" is from the phrase "jiéchū" (**excellent**) and "Míng" is from the phrase "cōngmíng"(**smart**).

李丽：没错！所以，"杰明"的**意思就是**"又杰出，又聪明"！是个**非常好**的名字！

Li Li: That's right! So "Jié Míng" **means** "excellent and smart!" It's an **extremely good** name!

杰明：是啊！我**知道**，在中国**文化**里，名字很**重要**，一定要有**意义**。

Jamie: True! I **know** that in Chinese **culture**, names are very **important** and must have **meanings**.

李丽：对！**所以**，你的名字很有**中国风**！

Li Li: Yes! **That's why** your name is very **Chinese style** (China wind)!

杰明：我很**幸运**！因为很多**外国朋友**的名字都是用**谷歌翻译**的，没有**意义**。

Jamie: I am very **lucky**! Because the names of many **foreign friends** are **translated by Google**, without any **meaning**.

李丽：**当然**，谷歌**很少**能翻译出有意义的名字。

Li Li: Of course, Google **rarely** translates names with meanings.

Learning Tip

Head over to my YouTube channel **LingLing Mandarin** where you can find videos to help you find a great Chinese name and other related learning videos.

Culture Corner

Localisation is extremely powerful when it comes to creating a Chinese name, whether it be for company or brand, or a personal name. This is because Chinese people ascribe great symbolic importance to names. So rather than using Google Translate which will produce typically meaningless Chinese names, it is far better to go for an authentic Chinese name; even better to have one that makes you stand out from the crowd (in a good way) and can be a great conversation starter!

An authentic Chinese name can be a smart localisation of your original name, or perhaps one with some personal meaning or relevance to you. It will help you establish your unique identity, reflect your personality, and help better engagement with your Chinese friends or business partners.

Chinese Name Service

Visit my website **www.linglingmandarin.com** find out more about the personalised Chinese Name Design service, if you're struggling to come up with your own.

Key Vocabulary

shí me shí hòu 什么时候		when / at what time	qù nián 去年	*n.*	last year
jué dé 觉得	*v.*	to think	zuì hǎo 最好	*adj.*	best
yī qǐ 一起	*adv.*	together	tè bié 特别	*adj.*	unique
qí shí 其实	*adv.*	actually	qǔ 取	*v.*	to pick
yì sī 意思	*n.*	meaning	wén huà 文化	*n.*	culture
zhòng yào 重要	*adj.*	important	zhōng guó fēng 中国风	*n.*	Chinese style
xìng yùn 幸运	*adj.*	lucky	fān yì 翻译	*v.*	to translate

Chinese Version

李丽：你和苏飞是什么时候认识的？

杰明：是去年六月份认识的。

李丽：我觉得你很喜欢她。

杰明：当然了！她是我在中国最好的朋友。

李丽：现在我和她也是朋友了，还经常一起吃饭。

杰明：是吗？这太棒了！

李丽：我觉得你的中文名字很特别！

杰明：其实，这个中文名字也是苏飞帮我取的。

李丽：那么，这个名字是什么意思呢？

杰明："杰"是"杰出"的"杰"，"明"是"聪明"的"明"。

李丽：没错！所以，"杰明"的意思就是"又杰出，又聪明"！是个非常好的名字！

杰明：是啊！我知道，在中国文化里，名字很重要，一定要有意义。

李丽：对！所以，你的名字很有中国风！

杰明：我很幸运！因为很多外国朋友的名字都是用谷歌翻译的，没有意义。

李丽：当然，谷歌很少能翻译出有意义的名字。

12

你有时间吗？
nǐ yǒu shí jiān ma
DO YOU HAVE TIME?

苏飞: 喂，丽丽！
sū fēi wéi lì lì

Su Fei: Hello, Li Li!

李丽: 喂，是飞飞吗？
lǐ lì wéi shì fēi fēi ma

Li Li: Hello, is that Feifei?

苏飞: 是啊，你在**忙什么**？
sū fēi shì ā nǐ zài máng shén me

Su Fei: Yes, **what** are you **up to**?

李丽: 没忙什么！现在在家里**看电视**呢，你打电话**有**
lǐ lì méi máng shén me xiàn zài zài jiā lǐ kàn diàn shì ne nǐ dǎ diàn huà yǒu

什么事吗？
shén me shì ma

Li Li: Nothing! Just **watching TV** at home now, **what's the matter** (you call me)?

苏飞: 呃，我**上次**说过明天会和你去**逛街**…
sū fēi è wǒ shàng cì shuō guò míng tiān huì hé nǐ qù guàng jiē

Su Fei: Uh, I mentioned **last time** that I would **go shopping** with you
     tomorrow...

李丽: 对啊！怎么了？
lǐ lì duì ā zěn me le

Li Li: Indeed! What's wrong?

sū fēi zhēn duì bù qǐ   wǒ míng tiān hěn máng   lái bù liǎo

苏飞:真对不起，我明天很忙，来不了。

Su Fei: I'm so **sorry**, I'm very **busy** tomorrow and can't come.

lǐ lì   ò   méi guān xì

李丽:哦，没关系。

Li Li: Oh, it doesn't matter.

sū fēi   bù guò   wǒ hòu tiān bù máng   nǐ yǒu shí jiān ma

苏飞:不过，我后天不忙，你有时间吗？

Su Fei: But, I am not busy **the day after tomorrow,** will you have **time**?

lǐ lì   yǒu   zhǐ shì   wǒ xià wǔ liǎng diǎn hòu cái yǒu shí jiān   kě yǐ ma

李丽:有！只是，我下午两点后才有时间，可以吗？

Li Li: Yes! **It's just** that I won't have time until **two o'clock in the afternoon**, is that okay?

sū fēi   dāng rán kě yǐ

苏飞:当然可以。

Su Fei: Of course.

lǐ lì   hǎo de   wǒ men kě yǐ xiān qù guàng jiē   rán hòu qù fàn guǎn chī fàn

李丽:好的。我们可以先去逛街，然后去饭馆吃饭。

Li Li: OK. We can go shopping **first**, and **then** eat in a restaurant.

sū fēi   hǎo ā   wǒ yǐ jīng hěn jiǔ méi qù guàng jiē le   zhēn de hěn xiǎng qù

苏飞:好啊！我已经很久没去逛街了，真的很想去。

Su Fei: Good! It **has been** a long time since I **went shopping**, I really want to go.

lǐ lì   wǒ zhī dào shì zhōng xīn de yī gè shū diàn   nà lǐ yǒu hěn duō xīn bǎn xiǎo
shuō   wǒ kě yǐ dài nǐ qù

**李丽:我知道市中心的一个书店，那里有很多新版小
说，我可以带你去。**

Li Li: I know a **bookstore** in the **city centre** with many new **novels**, I can take you there.

sū fēi   shū diàn lǐ kě yǐ hē chá ma

苏飞:书店里可以喝茶吗？

Su Fei: Can I **drink tea** in the bookstore?

lǐ lì   dāng rán kě yǐ   nà lǐ yǒu chá   yě yǒu qí tā yǐn liào

李丽:当然可以，那里有茶，也有其他饮料。

Li Li: Of course, there are **tea** and other **drinks**.

sū fēi   tài hǎo le   wǒ jiù xǐ huān yī biān kàn shū   yī biān hē chá   duì le
wǒ men hòu tiān zài nǎ lǐ jiàn miàn ne

**苏飞:太好了！我就喜欢一边看书，一边喝茶。对了，
我们后天在哪里见面呢？**

Su Fei: Great! I like to drink tea whilst I **read**. **By the way,** where shall we **meet** the day after tomorrow?

李丽：
lǐ lì wǒ xiǎngxiǎng wǒmen xià wǔ liǎng diǎn bàn zài dì tiě chū kǒu jiàn miàn
我想想，我们下午两点半在地铁B出口见面，
hǎo ma
好吗？

Li Li: Let me **have a think**. Let's meet at **Exit** B of the Metro at 2:30 in the afternoon, okay?

sū fēi hǎo de wǒ dào le huì gěi nǐ fā wēi xìn
苏飞：好的，我到了会给你**发微信**。

Su Fei: OK, I will **send** you a **WeChat message** when I arrive.

lǐ lì hǎo nà wǒmen hòu tiān jiàn
李丽：好！那我们**后天见**！

Li Li: Great! See you **the day after tomorrow**!

sū fēi hòu tiān jiàn
苏飞：后天见！

Su Fei: See you!

Learning Tip

wéi
喂 is a greeting which is typically used when answering a phone call in Chinese, it simply means "Hi" or "Hello" and can be used in a formal or informal context.

Culture Corner

In China, when people become friends, they usually stop calling one another by their full names, instead they just use given names or nicknames.

fēi fēi
As in the conversation, Li Li calls Su Fei 飞飞.

lì lì
Su Fei also calls Li Li 丽丽.

Key Vocabulary

diàn shì
电 视 *n.* TV

zěn me le
怎 么 了 *v.* what's wrong?

zhǐ shì
只 是 *adv.* just

rán hòu
然 后 *adv.* then

xīn bǎn
新 版 *n.* new (version)

yǐn liào
饮 料 *n.* drinks

xiǎng xiǎng
想　想 *v.* to have a think

guàng jiē
逛 街 *vp.* to go shopping

hòu tiān
后 天 *n.* the day after tomorrow

xiān
先 *adv.* first

shì zhōng xīn
市 中 心 *n.* city centre

shū diàn
书 店 *n.* bookshop

jiàn miàn
见 面 *v.* to meet up

chū kǒu
出 口 *n.* exit

58

Chinese Version

苏 飞：喂，丽丽！

李 丽：喂，是飞飞吗？

苏 飞：是啊，你在忙什么？

李 丽：没忙什么！现在在家里看电视呢，你打电话有什么事吗？

苏 飞：呃，我上次说过明天会和你去逛街……

李 丽：对啊！怎么了？

苏 飞：真对不起，我明天很忙，来不了。

李 丽：哦，没关系。

苏 飞：不过，我后天不忙，你有时间吗？

李 丽：有！只是，我下午两点后才有时间，可以吗？

苏 飞：当然可以。

李 丽：好的。我们可以先去逛街，然后去饭馆吃饭。

苏 飞：好啊！我已经很久没去逛街了，真的很想去。

李 丽：我知道市中心的一个书店，那里有很多新版小说，我可以带你去。

苏 飞：书店里可以喝茶吗？

李 丽：当然可以，那里有茶，也有其他饮料。

苏 飞：太好了！我就喜欢一边看书，一边喝茶。对了，我们后天在哪里见面呢？

李 丽：我想想，我们下午两点半在地铁B出口见面，好吗？

苏 飞：好的，我到了会给你发微信。

李 丽：好！那我们后天见！

苏 飞：后天见！

13 去 商 场 买 东 西
qù shāng chǎng mǎi dōng xī

GOING TO THE SHOPPING MALL

苏飞：李丽！我在**这儿**。
sū fēi   lǐ lì   wǒ zài zhè ér

Su Fei: Li Li! I'm **here**.

李丽：**嗨**，苏飞！你真**准时**。
lǐ lì   hēi   sū fēi   nǐ zhēnzhǔn shí

Li Li: **Hi**, Su Fei! You are so **punctual**.

苏飞：今天不**忙**，所以想**早点**来。
sū fēi   jīn tiān bù máng   suǒ yǐ xiǎng zǎo diǎn lái

Su Fei: I'm not **busy** today, so I wanted to come **earlier**.

李丽：我们**往前走**吧，先去**商场**，然后去**书店**。
lǐ lì   wǒ men wǎng qián zǒu ba   xiān qù shāngchǎng   rán hòu qù shū diàn

Li Li: Let's **walk ahead** to the **shopping mall** first, then we'll go to the **bookstore**.

苏飞：今天**天晴**，很**适合**逛街！
sū fēi   jīn tiān tiān qíng   hěn shì hé guàng jiē

Su Fei: So **sunny** today, **suitable** for going out shopping!

李丽：你看，那里在**卖**什么？
lǐ lì   nǐ kàn   nà lǐ zài mài shén me

Li Li: Look, what are they **selling** there?

苏飞：走，我们去看看。
sū fēi   zǒu   wǒ men qù kàn kàn

Su Fei: Let's go and see.

李丽：哇！好多**漂亮**的衣服，有**衬衫**、T恤、裤子和裙子。
Li Li:　Wow! So many **beautiful** clothes; **shirts**, T-shirts, trousers, and skirts.

苏飞：这件衬衫不错！你**觉得**哪个颜色**最好看**。
Su Fei: This shirt is good! Which colour do you **think** is **the best looking**?

李丽：我**觉得**蓝色和红色**都**好看，你呢？
Li Li:　I **think** blue and red **both** look good, what about you?

苏飞：我**更喜欢**红色，就买一件红色的吧！
Su Fei: I **prefer** (like more) red, I'll buy a red one!

李丽：我想买那条黄色的**裙子**，和我的白衬衫**很搭**。
Li Li:　I want to buy that yellow **skirt**. I think it **matches well** with my white shirt.

苏飞：嗯，我也觉得**很搭**！
Su Fei: Hmm, I also think they **match well**!

五分钟后...
5 minutes later...

李丽：那家**商店**在卖**手表**。你想去看看吗？
Li Li:　That **shop** sells **watches**. Do you want to have a look?

苏飞：我觉得手表**没什么用**。
Su Fei: I think watches **don't have much use**.

李丽：为什么？
Li Li:　Why?

苏飞：因为手机上也能**看时间**。
Su Fei: Because we can **check the time** on the phone.

李丽：是啊！**但是**，我觉得手表是很好的**礼物**，特别是
送给**男生**。
Li Li:　Yeah! **However**, I think watches are good **gifts**, especially for **guys**.

苏飞：你**这样说**，是不是有喜欢的**男生**了？

Su Fei: You **said this**, does it mean you have a **guy** you like?

李丽：别**开玩笑**了！我想买一个送**给**我爸爸，**下个月**
是他的**生日**。

Li Li: Stop **joking**! I want to buy one **for** my dad, **next month** is his **birthday**.

苏飞：嗯，是个**好主意**！我觉得他**一定**会喜欢。

Su Fei: Hmm, it's a **good idea**! I think he will **definitely** like it.

李丽：那我们**一起进去**看看吧。

Li Li: Let's **go in together** to have a look.

苏飞：好的。

Su Fei: Okay.

Key Vocabulary

zhǔn shí 准时	*adj.*	punctual		zǎo diǎn 早点	*adv.*	earlier
shāng chǎng 商场	*n.*	shopping mall		tiān qíng 天晴	*adj.*	sunny
shì hé 适合	*adj.*	suitable		mài 卖	*v.*	to sell
yī fú 衣服	*n.*	clothes		yán sè 颜色	*n.*	colour
hǎo kàn 好看	*adj.*	good-looking		dā 搭	*adj.*	well-matched
shǒu biǎo 手表	*n.*	watch		shì ā 是啊	*excl.*	yeah
lǐ wù 礼物	*n.*	gift		nán shēng 男生	*n.*	guy (male)
kāi wán xiào 开玩笑	*vp.*	to joke		zhǔ yì 主意	*n.*	idea

Chinese Version

苏飞：李丽！我在这儿。
李丽：嗨，苏飞！你真准时。
苏飞：今天不忙，所以想早点来。
李丽：我们往前走吧，先去商场，然后去书店。
苏飞：今天天晴，很适合逛街！
李丽：你看，那里在卖什么？
苏飞：走，我们去看看。
李丽：哇！好多漂亮的衣服，有衬衫、T恤、裤子和裙子。
苏飞：这件衬衫不错！你觉得哪个颜色最好看。
李丽：我觉得蓝色和红色都好看，你呢？
苏飞：我更喜欢红色，就买一件红色的吧！
李丽：我想买那条黄色的裙子，和我的白衬衫很搭。
苏飞：嗯，我也觉得很搭！

5分钟后...

李丽：那家商店在卖手表。你想去看看吗？
苏飞：我觉得手表没什么用。
李丽：为什么？
苏飞：因为手机上也能看时间。
李丽：是啊！但是，我觉得手表是很好的礼物，特别是送给男生。
苏飞：你这样说，是不是有喜欢的男生了？
李丽：别开玩笑了！我想买一个送给我爸爸，下个月是他的生日。
苏飞：嗯，是个好主意！我觉得他一定会喜欢。
李丽：那我们一起进去看看吧。
苏飞：好的。

14 在星巴克喝咖啡

zài xīng bā kè hē kā fēi

COFFEE IN STARBUCKS

苏飞：我走**累**了，想**休息一下**。
sū fēi wǒ zǒu lèi le xiǎng xiū xī yī xià

Su Fei: I'm **tired** of walking, I want to **take a short break**.

杰明：我也是。
jié míng wǒ yě shì

Jamie: Me too.

苏飞：你看，前面有家**咖啡馆**。啊！是**星巴克**。我们**进去**喝咖啡吧。
sū fēi nǐ kàn qiánmiàn yǒu jiā kā fēi guǎn ā shì xīng bā kè wǒ men jìn qù hē kā fēi ba

Su Fei: Look, there is a **cafe** in front. Ah! It's **Starbucks**. Let's **go in** for coffee.

到达星巴克...
dào dá xīng bā kè

Arriving at Starbucks...

杰明：我去**点**两杯咖啡。你想喝**什么**咖啡？
jié míng wǒ qù diǎn liǎng bēi kā fēi nǐ xiǎng hē shén me kā fēi

Jamie: I'll **order** two cups of coffee. **What** coffee would you like to drink?

苏飞：我**要**喝白咖啡，你呢？
sū fēi wǒ yào hē bái kā fēi nǐ ne

Su Fei: I **want to** drink white coffee, what about you?

杰明：我要喝黑咖啡。

Jamie: I **want to** drink black coffee.

杰明：你好！我要**一杯**白咖啡和**一杯**黑咖啡。

Jamie: Hello there! I want **a cup of** white coffee and **a cup of** black coffee.

服务员：好的。**一共**50元，请问你用**微信**还是**支付宝**？

Waitress: Okay. That comes to 50 Yuan **in total**, do you use **WeChat** or **Alipay**?

杰明：用微信吧。

Jamie: WeChat.

服务员：好的，请在这里**扫码**。

Waitress: Okay, please **scan the code** here.

两分钟后...

2 minutes later...

杰明：你的咖啡到了，这是**牛奶**和**糖**。

Jamie: Your coffee is here. This is **milk** and **sugar**.

苏飞：啊！谢谢你！

Su Fei: Ah! Thank you!

杰明：你**觉得**这里的咖啡怎么样？

Jamie: What do you **think of** the coffee here?

苏飞：我觉得**一般般**。不过，我很喜欢这里的**环境**，很
漂亮，也很**安静**。

Su Fei: I think it's **average**. However, I like the **environment** here, very beautiful and **quiet**.

杰明：我也是。而且，我**发现**这家咖啡店离我家很**近**。

Jamie: Me too. Besides, I **notice** this coffee shop is very **close** to my home.

66

苏飞：是啊！你从家走过来就10**分钟**。如果**骑自行车**，
更快！

Su Fei: Indeed! Just 10 **minutes** for you to walk from here to your home. If you **cycle**, it would be even faster!

杰明：我喜欢**走路，但是**更喜欢骑自行车！

Jamie: I like **walking, but** cycling is even better!

苏飞：我也是，上班、下班**都**骑自行车。

Su Fei: Me too. I **always** cycle to and from work.

杰明：这**周六**，我打算骑自行车去**人民公园**，你想**跟**
我去吗？

Jamie: This **Saturday**, I plan to cycle to the **People's Park**. Would you like to go **with** me?

苏飞：好啊！

Su Fei: Great!

Key Vocabulary

xiū xī yī xià 休息一下	*vp.*	to have a break	kā fēi guǎn 咖啡馆	*n.*	cafe
kā fēi 咖啡	*n.*	coffee	yī gòng 一共	*adv.*	in total
niú nǎi 牛奶	*n*	milk	táng 糖	*n.*	sugar
yī bān bān 一般般	*adj.*	average	huán jìng 环境	*n.*	environment
ān jìng 安静	*adj.*	quite	fā xiàn 发现	*v.*	to notice
jìn 近	*adj.*	close	fēn zhōng 分钟	*n.*	minutes
zǒu lù 走路	*v.*	to walk	shàng bān 上班	*v.*	to go to work / start work
xià bān 下班	*v.*	to get off work / finish work	dǎ suàn 打算	*v.*	to plan

Chinese Version

苏飞：我走累了，想休息一下。

杰明：我也是。

苏飞：你看，前面有家咖啡馆。啊！是星巴克。我们进去喝咖啡吧。

到达星巴克....

杰明：我去点两杯咖啡。你想喝什么咖啡？

苏飞：我要喝白咖啡，你呢？

杰明：我要喝黑咖啡。
    你好！我要一杯白咖啡和一杯黑咖啡。

服务员：好的。一共50元，请问你用微信还是支付宝？

杰明：用微信吧。

服务员：好的，请在这里扫码。

2分钟后...

杰明：你的咖啡到了，这是牛奶和糖。

苏飞：啊！谢谢你！

杰明：你觉得这里的咖啡怎么样？

苏飞：我觉得一般般。不过，我很喜欢这里的环境，很漂亮，也很安
    静。

杰明：我也是。而且，我发现，这家咖啡店离我家很近。

苏飞：是啊！你从家走过来就10分钟。如果骑自行车，更快！

杰明：我喜欢走路，但是更喜欢骑自行车！

苏飞：我也是，上班、下班都骑自行车。

杰明：这周六，我打算骑自行车去人民公园，你想跟我去吗？

苏飞：好啊！

15

疯 狂 的 网 购
fēng   kuáng   de   wǎng   gòu

CRAZY ONLINE SHOPPING

jié míng wǒ fā xiàn   zài zhōng guó wǎng gòu tài liú xíng le
杰明：我 **发现**，在 中 国 **网 购** 太 **流 行** 了！

Jamie: I've **noticed** that **online shopping** in China is very **popular**!

sū fēi   nǐ bù zhī dào ma zhōng guó shì shì jiè shàng zuì dà de wǎng gòu shì chǎng
苏飞：你 不 知 道 吗？中 国 是 **世 界 上** 最 大 的 **网 购 市 场**。

Su Fei: Don't you know that China is the largest **online shopping market in the world.**

jié míng zhēn de ma
杰明：真 的 吗？

Jamie: Really?

sū fēi dāng rán   zhè xiē nián   dà jiā dōu wǎng gòu wǎng gòu hěn pián yi xuǎn zé
苏飞：**当 然**！**这 些 年**，大 家 都 网 购。网 购 很 **便 宜**，**选 择**

            yě duō
     也 多。

Su Fei: Of course! **These years** almost everyone shops online. It's so **cheap** to buy things online and there are many **choices**.

jié míng zài zhōng guó   dà de wǎng gòu píng tái yǒu nǎ xiē
杰明：在 中 国，大 的 **网 购 平 台** 有 哪 些？

Jamie: What are the main **online shopping platforms** in China?

sū fēi dāng rán shì   jīng dōng hé   táo bǎo
苏飞：**当 然** 是 " 京 东 " 和 " 淘 宝 "。

Su Fei: **Of course**, it's "JD.com" and "Taobao".

jié míng　nǎ　gè　gèng hǎo
杰明：哪 个 更 好？

Jamie: Which is **better**?

sū fēi　wǒ jué dé dōu chà bù duō　yǒu xiē rén yòng　jīng dōng　yǒu xiē rén yòng
苏飞：我 觉 得 都 差 不 多，有 些 人 用"**京 东**"**，有 些 人 用**
táo bǎo　　hái yǒu yī xiē dōu yòng
"**淘 宝**"**，还 有 一 些 都 用**。

Su Fei: They're **more or less the same**. Some people **use** "JD.com", some use "Taobao", and some **use both**.

jié míng　nǐ　ne
杰明：你 呢？

Jamie: What about you?

sū fēi　wǒ yě dōu yòng　wǒ de shǒu jī shàng yǒu　jīng dōng　hé　táo bǎo　de
苏飞：我 也 都 用，我 的 手 机 上 有"**京 东**"**和**"**淘 宝**"**的**
shǒu jī chéng xù　nǐ kàn
手 机 程 序，你 看。

Su Fei: I use both **too**. I have **mobile apps** for "JD.com" and "Taobao" on my phone, see!

jié míng　nǐ jīn tiān chuān de xīn xié zǐ yě shì wǎng gòu de ma
杰明：你 今 天 穿 的 新 鞋 子 也 是 网 购 的 吗？

Jamie: Are the new **shoes** you are wearing today also bought online?

sū fēi　duì　zhè shì wǒ zuó tiān zài　jīng dōng shàng mǎi de　jīn tiān zǎo shàng jiù
苏飞：对！这 是 我 昨 天 在"**京 东**"**上 买 的，今 天 早 上 就**
dào le
到 了。

Su Fei: Yes! I bought them on "JD.com" **yesterday**, and they **arrived** this morning.

jié míng zěn me zhè me kuài
杰明：怎 么 这 么 快？

Jamie: **How could** it be so fast?

sū fēi　duì ā　yīn wèi　jīng dōng　de sù dù zuì kuài
苏飞：对 啊！因 为"**京 东**"**的 速 度 最 快**。

Su Fei: Indeed! Because the **speed** of "JD.com" is the fastest.

jié míng zhōng guó hěn dà　suǒ yǐ　wǒ jué dé hěn nán xiāng xìn yī tiān jiù dào le
杰明：中 国 很 大，所 以，我 觉 得 很 难 相 信 一 天 就 到 了。

Jamie: China is very big, **so** I find it hard to **believe** that it can arrive in one day.

sū fēi　qí shí　táo bǎo　sù dù yě kě yǐ　nǐ tóng xué men ne　yě huì
苏飞：其 实，"**淘 宝**"**速 度 也 可 以。你 同 学 们 呢，也 会**
wǎng gòu ma
网 购 吗？

Su Fei: **Actually**, the speed of "Taobao" is also **fine**. What about your **classmates**, do they also shop online?

jié míng tā men gèng fēng kuáng   tiān tiān wǎng gòu   tiān tiān shōu bāo guǒ
杰明:他们更疯狂，**天天**网购，天天**收包裹**。

Jamie: They are even crazier. They shop online **every day** and **receive packages** every day.

sū fēi   yuè   hào de wǎng gòu jié   cái shì zuì fēngkuáng de
苏飞:11月11号的**网购节**，才是最疯狂的。

Su Fei: Actually the **online shopping festival** on November 11 is the craziest.

jié míng duì   wǒ tīng shuō hěn duō dōng xī yě huì dǎ zhé
杰明:对！我**听说**很多东西也会**打折**。

Jamie: Yes! I **heard** that many things will also be **discounted**.

sū fēi   xià gè yuè jiù shì   yuè fèn le   nǐ zhǔn bèi hǎo le ma
苏飞:下个月就是11月份了，你**准备好**了吗？

Su Fei: **Next month** is November, are you **ready**?

jié míng dāng rán   wǒ jīn tiān jiù qù xià zǎi   jīng dōng   de shǒu jī chéng xù   shì
杰明:当然！我今天就去**下载**"京东"的**手机程序**，试
yī shì
一试。

Jamie: Of course! I'll **download** the "JD.com" **mobile app** today to **have a try**.

Culture Corner

Online shopping is the dominant shopping trend in China, which has become the largest online shopping market in the world. Taobao (owned by Alibaba) and JD.com are currently the two main platforms with several others growing fast although face tough competition.

Key Vocabulary

wǎng gòu 网购	*n.*	online shopping	liú xíng 流行	*adj.*	popular
shì jiè 世界	*n.*	world	shì chǎng 市场	*n.*	market
píng tái 平台	*n.*	platform	dāng rán 当然	*adv.*	of course
xié zǐ 鞋子	*n.*	shoes	sù dù 速度	*n.*	speed
suǒ yǐ 所以	*conj.*	so	xiāng xìn 相信	*v.*	to believe
tóng xué 同学	*n.*	classmates	tiān tiān 天天	*adv.*	everyday
fēng kuáng 疯狂	*adj.*	crazy	dǎ zhé 打折	*v.*	discount

Chinese Version

杰 明：我发现，在中国网购太流行了！

苏 飞：你不知道吗？中国是世界上最大的网购市场。

杰 明：真的吗？

苏 飞：当然！这些年，大家都网购。网购很便宜，选择也多。

杰 明：在中国，大的网购平台有哪些？

苏 飞：当然是"京东"和"淘宝"。

杰 明：哪个更好？

苏 飞：我觉得都差不多，有些人用"京东"，有些人用"淘宝"，还有一些都用。

杰 明：你呢？

苏 飞：我也都用，我的手机上有"京东"和"淘宝"的手机程序，你看。

杰 明：你今天穿的新鞋子也是网购的吗？

苏 飞：对！这是我昨天在"京东"上买的，今天早上就到了。

杰 明：怎么这么快？

苏 飞：对啊！因为"京东"的速度最快。

杰 明：中国很大，所以，我觉得很难相信一天就到了。

苏 飞：其实，"淘宝"速度也可以。你同学们呢，也会网购吗？

杰 明：他们更疯狂，天天网购，天天收包裹。

苏 飞：11月11号的网购节，才是最疯狂的。

杰 明：对！我听说很多东西也会打折。

苏 飞：下个月就是11月份了，你准备好了吗？

杰 明：当然！我今天就去下载"京东"的手机程序，试一试。

16

去 中 国 银 行
qù zhōng guó yín háng

GOING TO THE BANK OF CHINA

工作人员: gōng zuò rén yuán · xiān shēng nín hǎo xū yào bāngmáng ma
先生，您好！需要帮忙吗？
Staff: Hello, **sir**! Do you need **help**?

杰明: jié míng · nǐ hǎo wǒ yào bàn yī zhāng yín háng kǎ
你好！我要办一张银行卡。
Jamie: Hello! I would like to **apply for** a **bank card**.

工作人员: gōng zuò rén yuán · hǎo de qǐng gěi wǒ kàn nǐ de hù zhào
好的，请给我看你的护照。
Staff: Okay, please show me your **passport**.

杰明: jié míng · zhè shì hù zhào gěi nǐ
这是护照，给你。
Jamie: This is my passport, **here you are**.

工作人员: gōng zuò rén yuán · xiè xie qǐng wèn nín zài zhōng guó shì xué xí hái shì lǚ yóu
谢谢！请问您在中国是学习、还是旅游？
Staff: Thank you! May I ask are you **studying** or **traveling** in China?

杰明: jié míng · wèi shén me huì wèn zhè gè wèn tí
为什么会问这个问题？
Jamie: **Why** do you ask this **question**?

工作人员: gōng zuò rén yuán · yīn wèi yǒu xué xí qiānzhèng cái kě yǐ bàn yín háng kǎ rú guǒ shì
因为有学习签证，才可以办银行卡。如果是
lǚ yóu qiānzhèng jiù bù kě yǐ
旅游签证，就不可以。

Staff: **Because** you can only apply for a bank card if you have a **student visa**. If it is a **tourist visa**, we cannot help.

jié míng
杰明: 我的**签证**是学习签，签证**页**在护照里。

Jamie: My **visa** is a student visa, and the visa **page** is in the passport.

gōng zuò rén yuán
工作人员: 好的，我看看。请问你有**学生证**吗？

Staff: Okay, let me have a look. Do you have a **student ID card**?

jié míng
杰明: 有，在这儿。

Jamie: Yes, here it is.

gōng zuò rén yuán
工作人员: 谢谢！

Staff: Thank you!

jié míng
杰明: 对了，请你帮我开**网银**，这样**方便**在 网
shàng mǎi dōng xī
上**买东西**。

Jamie: Ah yes, please help me to open **online banking** so that I can **buy things** online **conveniently**.

gōng zuò rén yuán
工作人员: 可以，请**填表**。

Staff: That's fine, please **fill in the form**.

liǎng fēn zhōng hòu
两分钟后…

2 minutes later...

jié míng
杰明: 填好了，给你。

Jamie: It's done, here you are.

gōng zuò rén yuán
工作人员: 谢谢！请在这里**签字**。

Staff: Thank you, please **sign** here.

jié míng
杰明: 好的。

Jamie: Okay.

gōng zuò rén yuán
工作人员: 这是你的**银行卡**。请问**还有什么**需要吗？

Staff: Thank you! This is your **bank card**. Is there **anything else** I can help with?

jié míng
杰明： 我想用英镑换人民币，这是 100 英镑。
wǒ xiǎng yòng yīng bàng huàn rén mín bì   zhè shì   yīng bàng
Jamie: I would like to **exchange** pounds for RMB, here is 100 **pounds**.

gōng zuò rén yuán
工作人员： 好的，给您 880 块人民币。
hǎo de   gěi nín   kuài rén mín bì
Staff: Okay, here is 880 **RMB** for you.

jié míng
杰明： 谢谢你！再见！
xiè xie nǐ   zài jiàn
Jamie: Thank you! Goodbye!

gōng zuò rén yuán
工作人员： 再见！
zài jiàn
Staff: Goodbye!

Culture Corner

This is a travel tip for you - please note that you cannot typically apply for a bank card if you are a tourist in China, but you can if you are on a student or work visa. If you would like to shop online, you will also need to ask bank staff to activate online banking for you.

Key Vocabulary

xū yào 需要	*v.*	to need	bāng máng 帮忙	*n.*	help
bàn 办	*v.*	to apply	yín háng kǎ 银行卡	*n.*	bank card
hù zhào 护照	*n.*	passport	xué xí 学习	*v.*	study
lǚ yóu 旅游	*v.*	travel	wèn tí 问题	*n.*	question
qiān zhèng 签证	*n.*	visa	wǎng yín 网银	*n.*	online banking
tián biǎo 填表	*vp.*	to fill out a form	qiān zì 签字	*v.*	to sign
yīng bàng 英镑	*n.*	pound (currency)	rén mín bì 人民币	*n.*	RMB (the currency of Mainland China)

Chinese Version

工作人员：先生，您好！需要帮忙吗？

杰明：你好！我要办一张银行卡。

工作人员：好的，请给我看你的护照。

杰明：这是护照，给你。

工作人员：谢谢！请问您在中国是学习、还是旅游？

杰明：为什么会问这个问题？

工作人员：因为有学习签证，才可以办银行卡。如果是旅游签证，就不可以。

杰明：我的签证是学习签，签证页在护照里。

工作人民：好的，我看看。请问你有学生证吗？

杰明：有，在这儿。

工作人员：谢谢！

杰明：对了，请你帮我开网银，这样方便在网上买东西。

工作人员：可以，请填表。

2分钟后 …

杰明：填好了，给你。

工作人员：谢谢！请在这里签字。

杰明：好的。

工作人员：这是你的银行卡。请问还有什么需要吗？

杰明：我想用英镑换人民币，这是100英镑。

工作人员：好的，给您880块人民币。

杰明：谢谢你！再见！

工作人员：再见！

17

去 小 吃 街

qù xiǎo chī jiē

GOING TO THE FOOD STREET

苏飞：你看！这里就是我跟你说的**小吃街**。

sū fēi nǐ kàn zhè lǐ jiù shì wǒ gēn nǐ shuō de xiǎo chī jiē

Su Fei: Look! This is the **food street** I told you about.

杰明：哇，太香了！好多**美食**啊！

jié míng wā tài xiāng le hǎo duō měi shí ā

Jamie: Wow, it smells so good! So much **delicious food**!

苏飞：当然！这里的小吃又**便宜**又**好吃**！

sū fēi dāng rán zhè lǐ de xiǎo chī yòu pián yi yòu hǎo chī

Su Fei: Of course! Food here is **cheap** and **delicious**!

杰明：真是太**热闹**了！

jié míng zhēn shì tài rè nào le

Jamie: It's so **lively** too!

苏飞：对啊！**特别是**中午和晚上。

sū fēi duì ā tè bié shì zhōng wǔ hé wǎn shàng

Su Fei: Of course! **Especially** at noon and in the evening.

杰明：在英国，**下午五点半以后**，**多数**商店都**关门**了。

jié míng zài yīng guó xià wǔ wǔ diǎn bàn yǐ hòu duō shù shāng diàn dōu guān mén le

Jamie: In the UK, **most** shops are **closed** after 5:30 in the afternoon.

苏飞：在中国，**所有**的商店在五点半后，**最热闹**！

sū fēi zài zhōng guó suǒ yǒu de shāng diàn zài wǔ diǎn bàn hòu zuì rè nào

Su Fei: In China, **all** the shops are the **busiest** (most lively) after 5.30 pm.

80

杰明：我真喜欢这样的**生活**。对了，你**经常**来这里
jié míng wǒ zhēn xǐ huān zhè yàng de shēng huó duì le nǐ jīng cháng lái zhè lǐ

吃东西吗？
chī dōng xī ma

Jamie: I really like this kind of **life**. By the way, do you **often** come here to eat?

苏飞：是啊！我常常**下班**后来。
sū fēi shì ā wǒ cháng cháng xià bān hòu lái

Su Fei: Yes! I usually come after **finishing work**.

杰明：你**最喜欢**吃什么小吃？
jié míng nǐ zuì xǐ huān chī shén me xiǎo chī

Jamie: Which snack do you **like most**?

苏飞：我最喜欢吃**烤鱼**，你呢？
sū fēi wǒ zuì xǐ huān chī kǎo yú nǐ ne

Su Fei: I like **barbecued fish** the most, what about you?

杰明：我最喜欢吃**烤鸡腿**。
jié míng wǒ zuì xǐ huān chī kǎo jī tuǐ

Jamie: I love **barbecued chicken legs** the most.

苏飞：好！那今天我就**请你**吃烤鸡腿。
sū fēi hǎo nà jīn tiān wǒ jiù qǐng nǐ chī kǎo jī tuǐ

Su Fei: Great! Then I will **treat you** to barbecued chicken legs today.

杰明：哇！谢谢你！**看着**这些美食，我觉得快**饿死了**。
jié míng wā xiè xie nǐ kàn zhe zhè xiē měi shí wǒ jué dé kuài è sǐ le

Jamie: Wow! Thank you! I'm **starving looking at** all these food!

苏飞：你看，那里有个**烧烤摊**，我们过去吧。
sū fēi nǐ kàn nà lǐ yǒu gè shāo kǎo tān wǒ men guò qù ba

Su Fei: Look, there is a **barbecue stall** there, let's go over.

苏飞：老板，来**一份**烤鱼和**一份**烤鸡腿。
sū fēi lǎo bǎn lái yī fèn kǎo yú hé yī fèn kǎo jī tuǐ

Su Fei: Hi there (boss), I'd like **one** barbecued fish and **one** barbecued chicken leg.

摊主：好！一共25块，请在这里扫码**付款**！
tān zhǔ hǎo yī gòng kuài qǐng zài zhè lǐ sǎo mǎ fù kuǎn

Vendor: OK! That's 25 Yuan **in total**, please scan the code here **to pay**!

苏飞：好的。
sū fēi hǎo de

Su Fei: OK.

十分钟后...
shí fēn zhōng hòu

10 minutes later...

jié míng zhēn shì tài hǎo chī le   wǒ yǒu diǎn ér kě le xiǎng hē lěng yǐn   nǐ ne
杰明:真是太**好吃**了！我有点儿**渴**了，想喝**冷饮**，你呢？

Jamie: It's so **delicious**! I'm a little **thirsty** and feel like having a **cold drink**, what about you?

sū fēi   kě yǐ ā   gāng chī wán shāo kǎo   wǒ yě jué dé yǒu diǎn ér rè
苏飞:可以啊！**刚**吃完烧烤，我也觉得有点儿**热**！

Su Fei: Yes please! I **just** finished eating the barbecue, I feel a bit **hot** too!

jié míng   nà wǒ men qù mǎi liǎng bēi lěng yǐn ba
杰明:那我们去买**两杯**冷饮吧。

Jamie: Then let's go to buy **a couple of** cold drinks.

sū fēi   hǎo
苏飞:好！

Su Fei: Great!

jié míng   nǐ kàn   zhè tiáo jiē de hòu miàn yǒu gè lěng yǐn diàn   wǒ men guò qù ba
杰明:你看，这条**街**的后面有个**冷饮店**，我们过去吧。

Jamie: Look, there is a **cold drink shop** at the end of the **street**. Let's go over.

Culture Corner

In China it is normal to address vendors and shop and restaurant owners by calling them 老板 - the literal meaning is "boss." It is a colloquial term to address them politely.

Key Vocabulary

xiǎo chī jiē 小吃街	*n.*	food street	měi shí 美食	*n.*	delicious food / delicacy
rè nào 热闹	*adj.*	lively	tè bié 特别	*adv.*	especially
duō shù 多数	*n.*	most	guān mén 关门	*v.*	to close
suǒ yǒu 所有	*n.*	all	shēng huó 生活	*n.*	life
cháng cháng 常常	*adv.*	often	kě 渴	*adj.*	thirsty
lěng yǐn 冷饮	*n.*	cold drinks	rè 热	*adj.*	hot

Learning Tip

è sǐ le
饿 死 了 literally means "hungry to death" it is
used colloquially, similar to the use of "starving"
in English when used to exaggerate one's hunger.

sǐ le
死了 is commonly added after various adjectives in Chinese to
exaggerate the extent to which it applies, for example:

rè sǐ le
热 死 了　　hot to death

lěng sǐ le
冷 死 了　　cold to death

lèi sǐ le
累 死 了　　tired to death

Chinese Version

苏飞：你看！这里就是我跟你说的小吃街。

杰明：哇，太香了！好多美食啊！

苏飞：当然！这里的小吃又便宜又好吃！

杰明：真是太热闹了！

苏飞：对啊！特别是中午和晚上。

杰明：在英国，下午五点半以后，多数商店都关门了。

苏飞：在中国，所有的商店在五点半后，最热闹！

杰明：我真喜欢这样的生活。对了，你经常来这里吃东西吗？

苏飞：是啊！我常常下班后来。

杰明：你最喜欢吃什么小吃？

苏飞：我最喜欢吃烤鱼，你呢？

杰明：我最喜欢吃烤鸡腿。

苏飞：好！那今天我就请你吃烤鸡腿。

杰明：哇！谢谢你！看着这些美食，我觉得快饿死了。

苏飞：你看，那里有个烧烤摊，我们过去吧。
　　　　老板，来一份烤鱼和一份烤鸡腿。

摊主：好！一共25块，请在这里扫码付款！

苏飞：好的。

10 分钟后...

杰明：真是太好吃了！我有点儿渴了，想喝冷饮，你呢？

苏飞：可以啊！刚吃完烧烤，我也觉得有点儿热！

杰明：那我们去买两杯冷饮吧。

苏飞：好！

杰明：你看，这条街的后面有个冷饮店，我们过去吧。

18 你的狗真可爱！
nǐ de gǒu zhēn kě ài

YOUR DOG IS SO CUTE!

jié míng wā zhè shì nǐ de gǒu ma
杰明：哇！这是你的**狗**吗？
Jamie: Wow! Is this your **dog**?

lǐ lì shì de tā jiù shì wǒ jīng cháng gēn nǐ shuō de dà bǎo bèi
李丽：是的。它就是我**经常**跟你说的 "**大宝贝**"！
Li Li: Yes. It's the "**big baby**" I **often** mentioned to you!

jié míng zhēn kě ài tā jiào shén me míng zì
杰明：真**可爱**！它叫什么名字？
Jamie: He is so **cute**! What's his name?

lǐ lì tā jiào pàngpàng
李丽：它叫胖胖。
Li Li: He's called Fatty.

jié míng ng zhè gè míng zì hěn shì hé tā yīn wèi tā zhēn de yǒu diǎn ér pàng
杰明：嗯！这个名字很**适合**它。**因为**它真的有点儿**胖**！
Su Fei: Hmm! The name **suits** him well. **Because** he is indeed a bit **fat**!

lǐ lì duì wǒ jué dé pàng yī diǎn de gǒu gèng kě ài
李丽：对，我**觉得**胖一点的狗**更可爱**！
Li Li: Yes, I **think** fatter dogs are **cuter**!

jié míng tā jīn nián duō dà le
杰明：它今年**多大**了？
Jamie: **How old** is he?

<pre>
lǐ lì   wǔ suì bàn le
</pre>
李丽：五岁半了！

Li Li: Five and a half years old!

<pre>
jié míng   wǒ hěn xǐ huān tā de máo hěn ruǎn ér qiě shì wǒ zuì xǐ huān de bái
</pre>
杰明：我很喜欢它的毛，很软！而且是我最喜欢的白
<pre>
       sè hé zōng sè
</pre>
色和棕色。

Jamie: I really like his **fur**, it's soft! **Besides**, it's my favourite white and brown.

<pre>
lǐ lì   tā de máo tài duō le dōng tiān hái hǎo xià tiān hěn rè wǒ děi gěi tā
</pre>
李丽：它的毛太多了！冬天还好，夏天很热，我得给他
<pre>
       jiǎn máo
</pre>
剪毛。

Li Li: He has so much fur! It's okay for **winter**, but it's very hot for **summer** and I have to **cut** it for him.

<pre>
jié míng tā yī zhí kàn zhe wǒ   hǎo xiàng yě hěn xǐ huān wǒ
</pre>
杰明：它一直看着我，好像也很喜欢我。

Jamie: He **keeps** looking at me, **seems** to like me too.

<pre>
lǐ lì   dāng rán tā fēi cháng xǐ huān qīn jìn rén duì le nǐ yě yǒu gǒu ma
</pre>
李丽：当然！它非常喜欢亲近人！对了，你也有狗吗？

Li Li: Of course! He enjoys **being close to** people! **By the way**, do you have a dog too?

<pre>
jié míng méi yǒu   kě shì wǒ hěn xǐ huān xiǎo māo hé xiǎo gǒu
</pre>
杰明：没有，可是我很喜欢小猫和小狗。

Jamie: No, but I like **kittens** and **puppies** very much.

<pre>
lǐ lì   pàngpàng yǒu yī gè hǎo péng yǒu yě shì yī zhī māo tā men jīng cháng zài
</pre>
李丽：胖胖有一个好朋友，也是一只猫，它们经常在
<pre>
       yī qǐ wán
</pre>
一起玩。

Li Li: Fatty has a **good friend** who is also a cat. They often play **together**.

<pre>
jié míng pàngpàng zuì xǐ huān zuò shén me
</pre>
杰明：胖胖最喜欢做什么？

Jamie: What does Fatty like to do most?

<pre>
lǐ lì   tā zuì xǐ huān chī hé nǐ yī yàng shì gè chī huò
</pre>
李丽：它最喜欢吃，和你一样，是个 "吃货"！

Li Li: He likes to eat the most. **Just like you**, a "foodie"!

<pre>
jié míng hā hā   pàngpàng nǐ xiǎo xīn yuè chī yuè pàng
</pre>
杰明：哈哈！胖胖，你小心越吃越胖！

Jamie: Haha! Fatty, be careful **the more you eat, the fatter you get**!

<pre>
lǐ lì   tā yě fēi cháng hào dòng měi tiān zǎo shàng qǐ chuáng qǐ dé hěn zǎo
</pre>
李丽：它也非常好动，每天早上起床起得很早。

Li Li: He is also very **active** and **gets up** early every morning.

jié míng tā qǐ chuáng zuò shén me
杰明：它起床做什么？

Jamie: What does he do when he is up?

lǐ lì dāng rán shì děng zhe chī fàn yě děng zhe hé wǒ wán ér
李丽：当然是**等着**吃饭，也等着**和我玩儿**。

Li Li: Of course, **waiting** to eat and to **play with me**.

jié míng nà nǐ měi tiān zǎo shàng dōu huì bèi tā nòng xǐng ma
杰明：那你**每天早上**都会被它弄醒吗？

Jamie: So, **every morning** he wakes you up?

lǐ lì dāng rán le tā jiù xiàng wǒ de nào zhōng měi tiān zǎo shàng liù diǎn dōu huì
李丽：当然了！它就像我的**闹钟**，每天**早上六点**都会
qù wǒ de fáng jiān zhǎo wǒ
去我的**房间**找我。

Li Li: Of course! He's like my **alarm clock** and always goes to my **bedroom** to find me at **six every morning**.

Learning Tip

In Chinese, we only refer to humans with gender differences i.e. 他 (he) and 她 (she). For animals, we just use 它 (it). You can only tell their differences in written Chinese, there is no pronunciation difference of these characters in spoken Chinese.

Key Vocabulary

gǒu 狗	*n.*	dog	kě ài 可爱	*adj.*	cute
pàng 胖	*adj.*	fat	máo 毛	*n.*	hair/fur
ruǎn 软	*adj.*	soft	dōng tiān 冬天	*n.*	winter
xià tiān 夏天	*n.*	summer	jiǎn 剪	*v.*	to cut
yī zhí 一直	*adv.*	always/keep	hǎo xiàng 好像	*adv.*	seem
qīn jìn 亲近	*v.*	to be close to	wán 玩	*v.*	to play
yuè … yuè … 越…越…		the more…the more…	hào dòng 好动	*adj.*	active
qǐ chuáng 起床	*v.*	to get up	nào zhōng 闹钟	*n.*	alarm clock

Chinese Version

杰明：哇！这是你的狗吗？

李丽：是的。它就是我经常跟你说的大宝贝！

杰明：真可爱！它叫什么名字？

李丽：它叫胖胖。

杰明：嗯！这个名字很适合它。因为它真的有点儿胖！

李丽：对，我觉得胖一点的狗更可爱！

杰明：它今年多大了？

李丽：五岁半了！

杰明：我很喜欢它的毛，很软！而且是我最喜欢的白色和棕色。

李丽：它的毛太多了！冬天还好，夏天很热，我得给他剪毛。

杰明：它一直看着我，好像也很喜欢我。

李丽：当然！它非常喜欢亲近人！对了，你也有狗吗？

杰明：没有，可是我很喜欢小猫和小狗。

李丽：胖胖有一个好朋友，也是一只猫，它们经常在一起玩。

杰明：胖胖最喜欢做什么？

李丽：它最喜欢吃，和你一样，是个"吃货"！

杰明：哈哈！胖胖，你小心越吃越胖！

李丽：它也非常好动，每天早上起床起得很早。

杰明：它起床做什么？

李丽：当然是等着吃饭，也等着和我玩儿。

杰明：那你每天早上都会被它弄醒吗？

李丽：当然了！它就像我的闹钟，每天早上六点都会去我的房间找我。

19

去 茶 馆
qù chá guǎn

GOING TO THE TEAHOUSE

茶

sū fēi wǒ men dào le
苏飞：我们到了！
Su Fei: Here we are!

jié míng zhè jiā chá guǎn hěn yǒu zhōng guó fēng huán jìng hěn piāo liàng
杰明：这家**茶馆**很有**中国风**，环境很**漂亮**。
Jamie: This **teahouse** is very **Chinese style** and the environment is very **beautiful**.

sū fēi dāng rán le zhè lǐ yǒu zuì hǎo de zhōng guó chá
苏飞：当然了！这里有**最好的**中国茶。
Su Fei: Of course! It also has **the best** Chinese teas.

jié míng wǒ men xiān zuò xià ba nǐ kàn fú wù yuán lái le
杰明：我们先**坐下**吧。你看，**服务员**来了。
Jamie: Let's **sit down** first. Look, the **waitress** is coming.

fú wù yuán huān yíng guāng lín qǐng wèn nǐ men yào hē shén me chá
服务员：**欢迎光临**！请问你们要喝什么茶？
Waitress: Welcome! What kind of tea would you like to drink?

jié míng qǐng wèn nǐ men zhè lǐ yǒu nǎ xiē chá
杰明：请问，你们这里有**哪些**茶？
Jamie: May I ask **which** tea do you have here?

fú wù yuán wǒ men yǒu zhōng guó de shí dà míng chá zhè shì chá shuǐ dān
服务员：我们有中国的**十大名茶**，这是**茶水单**。
Waitress: We have **the ten famous teas** of China. This is the **tea list**.

杰明：我看看，我想喝**乌龙茶**，这个名字很**有意思**。

Jamie: Let me see, I want to drink **Oolong tea**, the name is very **interesting**.

苏飞：我也要**一杯**乌龙茶。

Su Fei: I also want **a cup of** Oolong tea.

服务员：好的，请你们**等一下**。

Waitress: Okay, please **wait a moment**.

苏飞：你**以前**喝过中国茶吗？

Su Fei: Have you ever had Chinese tea **before**?

杰明：当然！我最喜欢喝中国的**绿茶**和**红茶**，很健
康，也很**好喝**。

Jamie: Of course! I like to drink Chinese **green tea** and **red tea** the most, very
healthy and **tasty**.

苏飞：在**英国**的时候，你去**哪里**买中国茶？

Su Fei: **Where** did you buy Chinese tea when you were in the **UK**?

杰明：**有时候**去中国超市买，**有时候**在网上买。

Jamie: **Sometimes** from the Chinese supermarket, **sometimes** online.

服务员：这是你们的茶，**请慢用**！

Waitress: Here they are, **enjoy** (please slowly use)!

杰明：谢谢你！

Jamie: Thank you!

苏飞：这是**传统**的"**盖碗茶杯**"，你知道**怎么**用吗？

Su Fei: This is a **traditional** "gaiwan teacup". Do you know **how to** use it?

杰明：不知道，你可以**教**我吗？

Jamie: I don't know, can you **teach** me?

苏飞：可以！你看，**要这样**喝。

Su Fei: Yes! You see, just drink **like this**.

杰明：哦，我知道了。
jié míng   ò   wǒ zhī dào le

Jamie: Oh, I see.

苏飞：茶杯的**盖子代表**"天"、杯子**代表**"人"、**垫子**代
sū fēi   chá bēi de gài zǐ dài biǎo tiān   bēi zǐ dài biǎo rén   diàn zǐ dài
表"地"，意思是"**天地人合一**"，与**自然** 共
biǎo dì   yì sī shì   tiān dì rén hé yī   yǔ zì rán gòng
生！是一种 中国**哲学思想**。
shēng   shì yī zhǒng zhōng guó zhé xué sī xiǎng

Su Fei: The **lid** of the teacup **represents** "heaven", the cup **represents** "man", and the **saucer** represents "earth", it stands for "**the unity of heaven, earth, and man**" symbiosis with **nature**! This is a type of Chinese **philosophical thought**.

杰明：太**有趣**了！这样喝茶真是一种 **享受**。
jié míng   tài yǒu qù le   zhè yàng hē chá zhēn shì yī zhǒng xiǎng shòu

Jamie: It's so **interesting**! Drinking tea like this is truly an **enjoyment**.

苏飞：我有一本**关于** 中国茶**文化**的书，是 中英文的！
sū fēi   wǒ yǒu yī běn guān yú zhōng guó chá wén huà de shū   shì zhōng yīng wén de

Su Fei: I have a book **about** Chinese tea **culture**, in both Chinese and English!

杰明：可以**借**给我看看吗？
jié míng   kě yǐ jiè gěi wǒ kàn kàn ma

Jamie: Can you **lend** it to me?

苏飞：当然可以！
sū fēi   dāng rán kě yǐ

Su Fei: Of course!

Culture Corner

China has a profound tea culture with a long history. It's an art, as well as a lifestyle, and the drinking style varies depending on different tea-cups and tea sets. You should definitely go to try it when you visit China!

Key Vocabulary

chá guǎn
茶 馆   *n.*   tea house

fú wù yuán
服 务 员   *n.*   waiter/waitress

yǐ qián
以 前   *n.*   before(time)

hǎo hē
好 喝   *adj.*   tasty(drink)

chuántǒng
传 统   *adj.*   traditional

gài zǐ
盖 子   *n.*   lid

diàn zǐ
垫 子   *n.*   saucer

yǒu yì sī /
有 意 思 /
yǒu qù
有 趣   *adj.*   interesting

huán jìng
环 境   *n.*   environment

xiǎng shòu
享 受   *adj.*   enjoyable
       n.   enjoyment

jiàn kāng
健 康   *adj.*   healthy

wǎng shàng
网 上   *n.*   online

jiāo
教   *v.*   to teach

bēi zǐ
杯 子   *n.*   cup

zì rán
自 然   *n.*   nature

guān yú
关 于   *prep.*   about

Chinese Version

苏飞：我们到了！

杰明：这家茶馆很有中国风，环境很漂亮。

苏飞：当然了！这里有最好的中国茶。

杰明：我们先坐下吧。你看，服务员来了。

服务员：欢迎光临！请问你们要喝什么茶？

杰明：请问，你们这里有哪些茶？

服务员：我们有中国的十大名茶，这是茶水单。

杰明：我看看，我想喝乌龙茶，这个名字很有意思。

苏飞：我也要一杯乌龙茶。

服务员：好的，请你们等一下。

苏飞：你以前喝过中国茶吗？

杰明：当然！我最喜欢喝中国的绿茶和红茶，很健康，也很好喝。

苏飞：在英国的时候，你去哪里买中国茶？

杰明：有时候去中国超市买，有时候在网上买。

服务员：这是你们的茶，请慢用！

杰明：谢谢你！

苏飞：这是传统的盖碗茶杯，你知道怎么用吗？

杰明：不知道，你可以教我吗？

苏飞：可以！你看，要这样喝。

杰明：哦，我知道了。

苏飞：茶杯的盖子代表"天"、杯子代表"人"、垫子代表"地"，意思是"天地人合一"，与自然共生！是一种中国哲学思想。

杰明：太有趣了！这样喝茶真是一种享受。

苏飞：我有一本关于中国茶文化的书，是中英文的！

杰明：可以借给我看看吗？

苏飞：当然可以！

20 在手机上打车
zài shǒu jī shàng dǎ chē

ORDERING A TAXI BY PHONE

jié míng   fēi fēi   wǒ men děi chū fā le   nǐ kuài diǎn ér
杰明:飞飞，我们得**出发**了，你**快点儿**！

Jamie: Feifei, we have to **go** (set off), **hurry up**!

sū fēi   hǎo de   wǒ zài huàn yī fú   mǎ shàng jiù lái
苏飞:好的，我在**换衣服**，**马上**就来。

Su Fei: Okay, I'm **changing clothes**, will be there **right away**.

jié míng xiàn zài yǐ jīng liù diǎn bàn le   wǎn huì qī diǎn kāi shǐ   wǒ men zuò dì tiě
杰明:现在**已经**六点半了，**晚会**七点开始，我们坐地铁
qù   kě néng huì chí dào
去，可能会**迟到**。

Jamie: It's **already** half past six now. The **party** starts at seven. If we go by
metro, we might be **late**.

sū fēi   bié dān xīn   wǒ men kě yǐ dǎ chē qù   shí fēn zhōng jiù dào
苏飞:别**担心**，我们可以**打车**去，**十分钟**就到。

Su Fei: Don't **worry**, we can **take a taxi** and we'll arrive in ten **minutes**.

jié míng hǎo   nà wǒ men xiàn zài jiù qù wài miàn děng chū zū chē ba
杰明:好！那我们现在就去**外面**等**出租车**吧。

Jamie: Good! Let's go **outside** to wait for a **taxi** now.

sū fēi   bù yòng   wǒ zài jiā lǐ jiù kě yǐ dǎ chē
苏飞:不用，我**在家里**就可以打车。

Su Fei: **No need**, I can order a taxi here **at home**.

jié míng zhēn de ma　zěn me dǎ
杰明：真的吗？**怎么打**？

Jamie: Really? **How** to do it?

sū fēi　　nǐ kàn　　wǒ xià zǎi le shǒu jī chéng xù　　　dī dī chū xíng　　kě yǐ zài
苏飞：你看，我**下载**了**手机程序**"滴滴出行"，可以在
shàngmiàn dǎ chē
上面打车。

Su Fei: Look, I **downloaded** the **mobile app** "Didi Travel", and I can order a taxi on my phone.

jié míng　zhǐ yào yǒu wǎng　jiù kě yǐ zài rèn hé dì fāng　rèn hé shí jiān dǎ chē ma
杰明：**只要**有网，就可以在**任何地方**，**任何时间**打车吗？

Jamie: So **as long as** I have the internet, I can order a taxi from **anywhere** and **anytime**?

sū fēi　duì
苏飞：对！

Su Fei: Yes!

jié míng　zhè tài fāng biàn le
杰明：这太**方便**了。

Jamie: Wow! This is so **convenient**.

sū fēi　　nǐ kàn　　wǒ zài chéng xù shàng shū rù wǒ men de wèi zhì hé mù dì dì
苏飞：你看，我在程序上**输入**我们的**位置**和**目的地**，
rán hòu diǎn　hū jiào　　jiù kě yǐ le
然后**点**"**呼叫**"，就可以了。

Su Fei: You see, I **type in** our **location** and the **destination** to go on the mobile app, then **click** "Call", all done.

jié míng shàng miàn shuō yǒu sī jī yǐ jīng jiē dào　hū jiào　le　mǎ shàng jiù lái
杰明：上面说有**司机**已经接到"呼叫"了，**马上**就来！

Jamie: It says a **driver** has already received the call and will come **right away**!

sū fēi　duì　wǒ men hái kě yǐ kàn dào sī jī de wèi zhì
苏飞：对！我们还可以看到司机的**位置**。

Su Fei: Yes! We can also see the **location** of the driver too.

jié míng　ā　　hái yǒu sī jī de míng zì hé chē pái hào ne
杰明：啊！还有司机的名字和**车牌号**呢！

Jamie: Ah! And the driver's name and his **license plate number**!

sū fēi　duì　　sī jī liǎng fēn zhōng hòu jiù dào　wǒ men xiàn zài jiù xià lóu
苏飞：对！司机两分钟后就**到**，我们现在就**下楼**。

Su Fei: Yes! The driver will **arrive** in two minutes, let's **go downstairs** now.

jié míng duì le　　yī huì ér zěn me fù qián gěi sī jī
杰明：对了，一会儿怎么**付钱**给司机？

Jamie: By the way, how do we **pay** the driver later?

sū fēi bù yòng fù qián gěi sī jī wǒ men dào le mù dì dì hòu chéng xù huì
苏飞：不用**付钱**给司机。我们到了**目的地**后，程序会
zì dòng fù qián
自动付钱。

Su Fei: No need to **pay** the driver. When we arrive at our **destination**, payment will be **automatically** done through the app.

jié míng zhè gè shǒu jī chéng xù tài yǒu yòng le wǒ yě yào xià zǎi
杰明：这个手机程序太**有用**了，我也要**下载**。

Jamie: This app is so **useful**; I'll **download** it too.

Culture Corner

The most popular app used for taking a taxi in China is "Didi Travel." It is the easiest way to take a taxi for many Chinese people, and you don't even have to worry about paying them in person. Taxis can still be hailed from the street in major cities.

Key Vocabulary

chū fā 出 发	*v.*	to set off	kuài diǎn ér 快 点 儿			be quick
mǎ shàng 马 上	*adv.*	right away	wǎn huì 晚 会	*n.*		party
chí dào 迟 到	*adj.*	late	dǎ chē 打 车	*vp.*		take a taxi
zhǐ yào 只 要	*conj.*	as long as	rèn hé 任 何	*pro.*		any
shū rù 输 入	*v.*	to type in	mù dì dì 目 的 地	*n.*		destination
wèi zhì 位 置	*n.*	location	chē pái hào 车 牌 号	*n.*		plate number
fù qián 付 钱	*v.*	to pay	sī jī 司 机	*n.*		driver

Chinese Version

杰 明：飞飞，我们得出发了，你快点儿！

苏 飞：好的，我在换衣服，马上就来。

杰 明：现在已经六点半了，晚会七点开始，我们坐地铁去，可能会迟到。

苏 飞：别担心，我们可以打车去，十分钟就到。

杰 明：好！那我们现在就去外面等出租车吧。

苏 飞：不用，我在家里就可以打车。

杰 明：真的吗？怎么打？

苏 飞：你看，我下载了手机程序"滴滴出行"，可以在上面打车。

杰 明：只要有网，就可以在任何地方，任何时间打车吗？

苏 飞：对！

杰 明：这太方便了。

苏 飞：你看，我在程序上输入我们的位置和目的地，然后点"呼叫"，就可以了。

杰 明：上面说有司机已经接到呼叫了，马上就来！

苏 飞：对！我们还可以看到司机的位置。

杰 明：啊！还有司机的名字和车牌号呢！

苏 飞：对！司机两分钟后就到，我们现在就下楼。

杰 明：对了，一会儿怎么付钱给司机？

苏 飞：不用付钱给司机。我们到了目的地后，程序会自动付钱。

杰 明：这个手机程序太有用了，我也要下载。

21

去 健 身 房
qù jiàn shēn fáng

GOING TO THE GYM

jié míng   xià wǔ qù qí zì xíng chē   zěn me yàng
杰明: **下午**去**骑自行车**，怎么样？

Jamie: How about going **cycling** in the **afternoon**?

sū fēi   wǒ bù tài xiǎng qù   jīn tiān de tiān qì bù hǎo   yī huì ér kě néng huì
苏飞: 我不太想去！今天的**天气**不好！一会儿**可能**会
xià yǔ
下雨。

Su Fei: I don't really want to go! The **weather** is not good today! It'll **probably**
rain in a while.

jié míng   wǒ chá yī xià   jīn tiān xià yǔ   míng tiān tiān yīn   dàn shì hòu tiān tiān qíng
杰明: 我**查一下**，今天**下雨**，明天**天阴**，但是后天**天晴**。

Jamie: Let me **have a check**, it's **rainy** today and **cloudy** tomorrow, but the day
after tomorrow will be **sunny**.

sū fēi   nà wǒ men hòu tiān zài qù ba
苏飞: **那**我们**后天**再去吧。

Su Fei: **Then** let's go **the day after tomorrow**.

jié míng hǎo de   nǐ píng shí xǐ huān zuò shén me yùn dòng
杰明: 好的。你**平时**喜欢做什么**运动**？

Jamie: Okay. What **sports** do you **usually** like to do?

sū fēi   wǒ xǐ huān yóu yǒng   yě xǐ huān dǎ yǔ máo qiú hé pīng pāng qiú   nǐ ne
苏飞: 我喜欢**游泳**，也喜欢打**羽毛球**和**乒乓球**，你呢？

Su Fei: I like **swimming**. I also like playing **badminton** and **table tennis**. What
about you?

jié míng wǒ xǐ huān dǎ **wǎng qiú**   yě xǐ huān tī **zú qiú**
杰明：我 喜 欢 打 **网球**，也 喜 欢 踢 **足球**。
Jamie: I like playing **tennis** and **football**.

sū fēi duì le   nǐ qù **jiàn shēn fáng** ma
苏飞：对 了，你 去 **健身房** 吗？
Su Fei: By the way, do you go to the **gym**?

jié míng wǒ zǎo jiù xiǎng qù le   **dàn shì** hái méi yǒu zhǎo dào **hé shì** de
杰明：我 早 就 想 去 了，**但是** 还 没 有 找 到 **合适** 的。
Jamie: I really want to go, **but** I haven't found a **suitable** one.

sū fēi wǒ zhī dào yī jiā **jiàn shēn fáng**   jiù zài nǐ xué xiào **páng biān**
苏飞：我 知 道 一 家 **健身房**，就 在 你 学 校 **旁边**。
Su Fei: I know a **gym**, right **next to** your campus.

jié míng shì ma   kě yǐ **jiè shào** gěi wǒ ma
杰明：是 吗？可 以 **介绍** 给 我 吗？
Jamie: Really? Can you **introduce** it to me?

sū fēi **dāng rán**   nǐ kàn   zhè shì wǒ de **huì yuán kǎ**   wǒ jīn tiān xià wǔ qù nà
苏飞：**当然**！你 看，这 是 我 的 **会员卡**。我 今 天 下 午 去 那
lǐ **jiàn shēn**   nǐ hé wǒ qù **kàn kàn** ba
里 **健身**，你 和 我 去 **看看** 吧！
Su Fei: Of course! Look, this is my **membership card**. I'm going there to
exercise this afternoon. Go with me and **take a look**!

jié míng tài hǎo le   **duì le**   nǐ de huì yuán kǎ **yī gè yuè** duō shǎo qián
杰明：太 好 了！**对了**，你 的 会 员 卡 **一个月** 多 少 钱？
Jamie: That's great! **By the way**, how much is your membership card **per month**?

sū fēi yī gè yuè **cái**   kuài qián   bù **guì**
苏飞：一 个 月 **才** 30 块 钱，不 **贵**！
Su Fei: **Only** 30 Yuan per month, not **expensive**!

jié míng **hé** yīng guó de **bǐ**   zhè zhēn de tài pián yi le
杰明：**和** 英 国 的 **比**，这 真 的 太 便 宜 了！
Jamie: **Compared with** the UK, that is really **cheap**!

sū fēi shì ā
苏飞：是 啊！
Su Fei: Indeed!

jié míng nǐ shì **cóng shén me shí hòu** kāi shǐ qù **jiàn shēn fáng** de
杰明：你 是 **从什么时候** 开 始 去 **健身房** 的？
Jamie: **When** did you start to go to the **gym**?

sū fēi **cóng shàng gè yuè**   **dàn shì** huì yuán kǎ shì **shàng zhōu** cái bàn de
苏飞：**从 上 个 月**，**但是** 会 员 卡 是 **上周** 才 办 的。
Su Fei: **From** last month, **but** I didn't apply for the membership card until **last
week**.

jié míng wǒ yě xiǎng qù bàn yī zhāng xiǎng yào shēn tǐ hǎo　　jiù yào duō yùn dòng
杰明：我 也 想 去 **办** 一 张 。想 要 **身 体 好**，就 要 **多 运 动**！

Jamie: I also want to **apply for** one. If you want to be **healthy** (body good), you have to **exercise more**!

Key Vocabulary

tiān qì 天 气	*n.*	weather		xià yǔ 下 雨	*v.*	to rain
tiān yīn 天 阴	*adj.*	cloudy		tiān qíng 天 晴	*adj.*	sunny
píng shí 平 时	*adv.*	usually		yùn dòng 运 动	*n.*	sports
yóu yǒng 游 泳	*v.*	to swim		yǔ máo qiú 羽 毛 球	*n.*	badminton
pīngpāng qiú 乒 乓 球	*n.*	table tennis		wǎng qiú 网 球	*n.*	tennis
zú qiú 足 球	*n.*	football		jiàn shēn fáng 健 身 房	*n.*	gym
jiè shào 介 绍	*v.* *n.*	to introduce introduction		huì yuán 会 员	*n.*	membership
hé … bǐ 和 … 比	*vp.*	compare with …		shēn tǐ 身 体	*n.*	health

Chinese Version

杰明：下午去骑自行车，怎么样？

苏飞：我不太想去！今天的天气不好！一会儿可能会下雨。

杰明：我查一下，今天下雨，明天天阴，但是后天天晴。

苏飞：那我们后天再去吧。

杰明：好的。你平时喜欢做什么运动？

苏飞：我喜欢游泳，也喜欢打羽毛球和乒乓球，你呢？

杰明：我喜欢打网球，也喜欢踢足球。

苏飞：对了，你去健身房吗？

杰明：我早就想去了，但是还没有找到合适的。

苏飞：我知道一家健身房，就在你学校旁边。

杰明：是吗？可以介绍给我吗？

苏飞：当然！你看，这是我的会员卡。我今天下午去那里健身，你和我
　　　去看看吧！

杰明：太好了！对了，你的会员卡一个月多少钱？

苏飞：一个月才30块钱，不贵！

杰明：和英国的比，这真的太便宜了！

苏飞：是啊！

杰明：你是从什么时候开始去健身房的？

苏飞：从上个月，但是会员卡是上周才办的。

杰明：我也想去办一张。想要身体好，就要多运动！

22 到 北 京 机 场 了
dào　　bĕi　　jīng　　jī　　chǎng　　le

ARRIVING AT BEIJING AIRPORT

jié míng　dào bĕi jīng　jī chǎng le
杰明：到北京机场了！

Jamie: (We have) arrived at Beijing **Airport**!

sū fēi　shì ā　　cóngshàng hǎi dào bĕi jīng　　zuò fēi jī jiù liǎng gè bàn xiǎo shí
苏飞：是啊！从上海到北京，坐飞机就两个半小时。

Su Fei: Indeed! **From** Shanghai **to** Beijing, it takes only two and a half hours **by
plane**.

jié míng　xiàn zài　jǐ diǎn le
杰明：现在几点了？

Jamie: What's time now?

sū fēi　　wǔ diǎn bàn
苏飞：五点半。

Su Fei: Five thirty.

jié míng　wǒ men zài bĕi jīng de zhè sān tiān　　xíngchéng shì shén me
杰明：我们在北京的这三天，行程是什么？

Jamie: What is our **itinerary** in Beijing these three days?

sū fēi　jīn tiān xiū xī　míng tiān qù pá chángchéng　hòu tiān qù gù gōng
苏飞：今天休息，明天去爬长城，后天去故宫。

Su Fei: We'll **rest** today. Tomorrow we'll climb **the Great Wall**, and the day after
tomorrow we will go to **the Forbidden City**.

jié míng　xiàn zài shì qiū tiān　　pá chángchéng zuì hé shì　bù lěng　yě bù rè
杰明：现在是秋天，爬长城最合适。不冷，也不热！

Jamie: It's **autumn** now, good time to climb the Great Wall. It's neither **cold** nor **hot**!

<ruby>苏 su fēi 飞</ruby>：是啊！北京的春天和秋天**最凉快**、**最舒服**。

sū fēi shì ā běi jīng de chūn tiān hé qiū tiān zuì liáng kuài zuì shū fú

Su Fei: Indeed! Spring and autumn in Beijing are the **coolest** and **most comfortable**.

jié míng hái yǒu wǒ men shì xīng qī tiān zuò gāo tiě huí shàng hǎi ma
杰明：**还有**，我们是星期天**坐高铁**回上海吗？

Jamie: **Also**, will we return to Shanghai **by high-speed train** on Sunday?

sū fēi duì nǐ yǐ jīng mǎi le gāo tiě piào bù shì ma
苏飞：对！你已经买了**高铁票**，不是吗？

Su Fei: Yes! I remember you already bought the **high-speed train tickets**, didn't you?

jié míng shì de cóng běi jīng dào shàng hǎi zuò gāo tiě yào gè xiǎo shí suī rán
杰明：是的。从北京到上海，坐高铁要4个**小时**。**虽然**
shí jiān yǒu diǎn cháng dàn shì bù yòng huā shí jiān děng chē
时间有点**长**，但是不用**花时间**等车。

Jamie: Yes. From Beijing to Shanghai, it takes 4 **hours** by high-speed train. **Although** the time is a bit **long**, we don't have to **spend time** waiting for it.

sū fēi shì ā ér qiě gāo tiě hěn shū fú wǒ men hái kě yǐ kàn fēng jǐng
苏飞：是啊！而且**高铁**很舒服，我们还可以**看风景**。

Su Fei: Indeed! Plus the **high-speed train** is also very comfortable, we can **see the scenery** too.

jié míng nǐ yǐ qián lái guò běi jīng ma
杰明：你以前**来过**北京吗？

Jamie: **Have** you **been to** Beijing before?

sū fēi lái guò wǒ xiǎo de shí hòu cháng cháng hé fù mǔ lái běi jīng lǚ yóu
苏飞：来过，我小的时候，**常常**和**父母**来北京旅游。

Su Fei: Yes, I have. When I was little, I **often** travelled to Beijing with my **parents**.

jié míng nǐ kàn nà shì wǒ men de xíng lǐ xiāng wǒ men qù ná ba
杰明：你看，那是我们的**行李箱**，我们去拿吧。

Jamie: Look, those are our **luggage cases**. Let's **get** them.

sū fēi xíng lǐ tài duō le wǒ men dǎ chū zū chē ba
苏飞：**行李**太多了！我们**打出租车**吧。

Su Fei: Too much **luggage**! Let's **take a taxi**.

jié míng hǎo de nǐ xiān xiū xī yī xià wǒ yòng shǒu jī jiào chū zū chē
杰明：好的。你**先**休息一下，我用手机**叫出租车**。

Jamie: Okay. You take a rest here **first**. I will use my phone to **call** a taxi.

sū fēi　zhè lǐ　bù yòng jiào chē　　yīn wèi jī chǎng de chū zū chē tài duō le　　chū

苏飞：这里**不用**叫车，**因为**机场的**出租车**太多了，**出**

mén jiù néngshàng chē

门就能上车。

Su Fei: There is **no need** to call a taxi here, **because** there are so many **taxis** at the airport and we can get one straight away when we **go out**.

jié míng　hǎo de

杰明：好的。

Jamie: Okay.

sū fēi　　wǒ men xiàn zài jiù zuò chē qù bīn guǎn xiū xī yī xià

苏飞：我们**现在**就坐车去**宾馆**休息一下。

Su Fei: **Now** let's take the taxi to the **hotel** to have a rest.

liǎng fēn zhōng hòu

两分钟后...

2 minutes later...

sū fēi　shī fù　　nǐ hǎo　　wǒ men qù yángguāng bīn guǎn

苏飞：师傅，你好！我们去**阳光宾馆**。

Su Fei: Hello, there! We are going to the **Sunshine Hotel**.

sī jī　hǎo de　　qǐngshàng chē

司机：好的，请**上车**。

Driver: Okay, please **get in** the car.

Culture Corner

The most common way to address drivers in
shī fù
Chinese is 师傅, which literally means "master",
but this is just a colloquial term of polite addressing.

Key Vocabulary

jī chǎng 机 场	*n.*	airport		zuò fēi jī 坐 飞 机	*vp.*	to take an airplane / go by airplane
xíng chéng 行 程	*n.*	itinerary		xiū xī 休 息	*v.*	to rest
qiū tiān 秋 天	*n.*	autumn		liáng kuài 凉 快	*adj.*	cool
chūn tiān 春 天	*n.*	spring		shū fú 舒 服	*adj.*	comfortable
fēng jǐng 风 景	*n.*	scenery		fù mǔ 父 母	*n.*	parents
lǚ yóu 旅 游	*v.*	to travel		xíng lǐ xiāng 行 李 箱	*n.*	suitcase
yīn wèi 因 为	*conj.*	because		bīn guǎn 宾 馆	*n.*	hotel

Chinese Version

杰明：到北京机场了！

苏飞：是啊！从上海到北京，坐飞机就两个半小时。

杰明：现在几点了？

苏飞：五点半。

杰明：我们在北京的这三天，行程是什么？

苏飞：今天休息，明天去爬长城，后天去故宫。

杰明：现在是秋天，爬长城最合适。不冷，也不热！

苏飞：是啊！北京的春天和秋天最凉快、最舒服。

杰明：还有，我们是星期天坐高铁回上海吗？

苏飞：对！你已经买了高铁票，不是吗？

杰明：是的。从北京到上海，坐高铁要4个小时。虽然时间有点长，但是不用花时间等车。

苏飞：是啊！而且高铁很舒服，我们还可以看风景。

杰明：你以前来过北京吗？

苏飞：来过，我小的时候，常常和父母来北京旅游。

杰明：你看，那是我们的行李箱，我们去拿吧。

苏飞：行李太多了！我们打出租车吧。

杰明：好的。你先休息一下，我用手机叫出租车。

苏飞：这里不用叫车，因为机场的出租车太多了，出门就能上车。

杰明：好的。

苏飞：我们现在就坐车去宾馆休息一下。

2分钟后...

苏飞：师傅，你好！我们去阳光宾馆。

司机：好的，请上车。

23 去宾馆登记
qù bīn guǎn dēng jì
CHECKING INTO THE HOTEL

sū fēi
苏飞：
Su Fei:
zhōng yú dào le   wǒ men qù qián tái dēng jì ba
终于到了！我们去前台**登记**吧。
We are **finally** here! Let's go to the counter to **check-in**.

jié míng
杰明：
Jamie:
hǎo de   zhè gè bīn guǎn zhēn piào liàng
好的，这个**宾馆**真漂亮！
Okay, this **hotel** is so beautiful!

gōng zuò rén yuán
工作人员：
Staff:
nǐ men hǎo   huān yíng guāng lín
你们好！**欢迎光临**！
Hello! **welcome**!

jié míng
杰明：
nǐ hǎo   zhè shì wǒ men de fáng jiān dìng dān   yǐ jīng zài wǎng
你好！这是我们的**房间订单**，已经在网
shàng wán chéng zhī fù le
上**完成**支付了。
Jamie:
Hello! This is our **room-booking order**, with the payment already **completed** online.

gōng zuò rén yuán   hǎo de   wǒ kàn yī xià   nǐ men dìng de shì liǎng gè dān rén jiān
工作人员：好的，我**看一下**。你们订的是两个**单人间**，
duì ma
对吗？
Staff:
Okay, let me **have a look**. You booked two **single rooms**, right?

jié míng
杰明：
duì
对。
Jamie:
Yes.

109

gōng zuò rén yuán　xiè xie　　qǐng wèn nǐ men de míng zì shì
工作人员：谢谢！请问你们的名字是？
Staff:　　　　　Thank you! What are your names?

jié míng　　　　wǒ jiào jié míng　　tā jiào sū fēi
杰明：　　我叫杰明，她叫苏飞。
Jamie:　　　　　I am Jamie and her name is Su Fei.

gōng zuò rén yuán　xiè xie　　qǐng gěi wǒ kàn nǐ men de hù zhào hé shēn fèn zhèng
工作人员：谢谢！请给我看你们的**护照**和**身份证**。
Staff:　　　　　Thank you! Please show me your **passport** and **ID card**.

jié míng　　　　zhè shì wǒ de hù zhào
杰明：　　这是我的**护照**。
Jamie:　　　　　This is my **passport**.

sū fēi　　　　　zhè shì wǒ de shēn fèn zhèng　gěi nǐ
苏飞：　　这是我的**身份证**，给你。
Su Fei:　　　　　This is my **ID card**, here you are.

gōng zuò rén yuán　xiè xie　　qǐng wèn　　nǐ men yī gòng huì zài bīn guǎn zhù sān tiān
工作人员：谢谢！请问，你们**一共**会在宾馆住三天，
　　　　　　　duì ma
　　　　　　　对吗？
Staff:　　　　　Thank you! May I confirm, you will stay in the hotel for three days
　　　　　　　in total, right?

jié míng　　　　duì
杰明：　　对。
Jamie:　　　　　Yes.

gōng zuò rén yuán　xiǎo jiě　　nín de fáng jiān hào mǎ shì　　　zhè shì nín de fáng kǎ
工作人员：小姐，您的**房间号码**是715，这是您的**房卡**。
Staff:　　　　　Miss, your **room number** is 715, this is your **room card**.

sū fēi　　　　　xiè xie
苏飞：　　谢谢！
Su Fei:　　　　　Thank you!

gōng zuò rén yuán　xiān shēng　　nín de fáng jiān hào mǎ shì　　　zhè shì nín de fáng kǎ
工作人员：先生，您的**房间号码**是720，这是您的**房卡**。
Staff:　　　　　Sir, your **room number** is 720, this is your **room card**.

jié míng　　　　xiè xie nǐ
杰明：　　谢谢你！
Jamie:　　　　　Thank you!

gōng zuò rén yuán　bù kè qì　　cān tīng zài yī lóu　zǎo fàn de shí jiān shì cóng　diǎn
工作人员：不客气。**餐厅**在一楼，**早饭**的时间是从7点
　　　　　　　dào　　diǎn　　qǐng wèn hái yǒu shén me wèn tí ma
　　　　　　　到10点。请问还有什么**问题**吗？

Staff: You are welcome. The **dining hall** is on the first floor, and **breakfast** is from 7 to 10 o'clock. Do you have any **questions**?

sū fēi
苏飞： 没有了，谢谢你！
méi yǒu le　xiè xie nǐ
Su Fei: No, thank you!

gōng zuò rén yuán
工作人员： 祝你们在北京玩得开心！
zhù nǐ men zài běi jīng wán dé kāi xīn
Staff: May you **have a great time** in Beijing!

jié míng
杰明： 谢谢！再见。
xiè xie　zài jiàn
Jamie: Thank you! Goodbye.

sū fēi
苏飞： 电梯在那儿，我们现在去房间休息一下。
diàn tī zài nà ér　wǒ men xiàn zài qù fáng jiān xiū xī yī xià
Su Fei: The **elevator** is there. Let's go to the room to **take a rest** now.

jié míng
杰明： 好的，我想先去洗澡，大概要20分钟。
hǎo de　wǒ xiǎng xiān qù xǐ zǎo　dà gài yào　fēn zhōng
Jamie: Okay, I want to **take a shower** first, give me **about** 20 minutes.

sū fēi
苏飞： 可以！我们半小时后，再出发去天安门广
kě yǐ　wǒ men bàn xiǎo shí hòu　zài chū fā qù tiān ān mén guǎng
场。
chǎng
Su Fei: **Sure!** Then we will go to **Tiananmen Square** in half an hour.

jié míng
杰明： 好！
hǎo
Jamie: Great!

Culture Corner

Checking in to a hotel in China requires ID. Non-Chinese citizens are required to provide a passport. Whereas Chinese citizens must show their national ID card. Without these, it is likely that the hotel will refuse to allow check-in.

Key Vocabulary

dēng jì 登记	v.	to check-in	dìng dān 订单	n.	booking order
zhī fù 支付	v.	to pay	dān rén jiān 单人间	n.	single room
biāo zhǔn jiān 标准间	n.	standard room	shuāng rén jiān 双人间	n.	double room
hù zhào 护照	n.	passport	yī gòng 一共	adv.	in total
hào mǎ 号码	n.	number	fáng kǎ 房卡	n.	room card
cān tīng 餐厅	n.	dining hall	zǎo fàn 早饭	n.	breakfast
diàn tī 电梯	n.	elevator	xǐ zǎo 洗澡	v.	to shower
dà gài 大概	adv.	about	guǎng chǎng 广场	n.	square

Chinese Version

苏飞：终于到了！我们去前台登记吧。

杰明：好的，这个宾馆真漂亮！

工作人员：你们好！欢迎光临！

杰明：你好！这是我们的房间订单，已经在网上完成支付了。

工作人员：好的，我看一下。你们订的是两个单人间，对吗？

杰明：对。

工作人员：谢谢！请问你们的名字是？

杰明：我叫杰明，她叫苏飞。

工作人员：谢谢！请给我看你们的护照和身份证。

杰明：这是我的护照。

苏飞：这是我的身份证，给你。

工作人员：谢谢！请问，你们一共会在宾馆住三天，对吗？

杰明：对。

工作人员：小姐，您的房间号码是715，这是您的房卡。

苏飞：谢谢！

工作人员：先生，您的房间号码是720，这是您的房卡。

杰明：谢谢你！

工作人员：不客气。餐厅在一楼，早饭的时间是从7点到10点。请问还有什么问题吗？

苏飞：没有了，谢谢你！

工作人员：祝你们在北京玩得开心！

杰明：谢谢！再见。

苏飞：电梯在那儿，我们现在去房间休息一下。

杰明：好的，我想先去洗澡，大概要20分钟。

苏飞：可以！我们半小时后，再出发去天安门广场。

杰明：好！

24

生 日 快 乐 !
shēng rì kuài lè

HAPPY BIRTHDAY!

苏飞：杰明，祝你 **生日快乐**！
sū fēi   jié míng   zhù nǐ shēng rì kuài lè
Su Fei: Jamie, **happy birthday** to you!

杰明：谢谢你！
jié míng   xiè xie nǐ
Jamie: Thank you!

苏飞：不客气！这是送给你的 **生日礼物**。
sū fēi   bù kè qì   zhè shì sòng gěi nǐ de shēng rì lǐ wù
Su Fei: You're welcome! This is a **birthday gift** for you.

杰明：哇！**看上去**真漂亮！我可以现在 **打开** 吗？
jié míng   wā   kàn shàng qù zhēn piāo liàng   wǒ kě yǐ xiàn zài dǎ kāi ma
Jamie: Wow! It **looks** so beautiful! Can I **open** it now?

苏飞：唔，不可以！
sū fēi   wú   bù kě yǐ
Su Fei: Well, not really!

杰明：为什么？
jié míng   wèi shén me
Jamie: Why?

苏飞：因为在中国，我们收到礼物 **的时候**，一般不可
sū fēi   yīn wèi zài zhōng guó   wǒ men shōu dào lǐ wù de shí hòu   yī bān bù kě
以 **马上** 打开。
yǐ mǎ shàng dǎ kāi

Su Fei: Because in China, **when** we receive a gift, we usually don't open it **straight away**.

jié míng nà wǒ shén me shí hòu cái kě yǐ dǎ kāi
杰明：那 我 什 么 时 候 **才** 可 以 **打开**？
Jamie: Then when can I **open** it?

sū fēi děngshēng rì jù huì jié shù yǐ hòu   nǐ cái kě yǐ dǎ kāi
苏飞：等 生 日 聚会 结 束 以 后 ，你 **才** 可 以 打 开 。
Su Fei: You can **only** open it when the **birthday party** is over.

jié míng hǎo ba
杰明：好 吧。
Jamie: Okay.

sū fēi cóng jīn tiān kāi shǐ   nǐ jiù   suì le   gǎn jué zěn me yàng
苏飞：从 今 天 开 始，你 就 ２７岁 了 ，**感觉** 怎 么 样 ？
Su Fei: From today, you are 27 years old. How do you **feel**?

jié míng gǎn jué shí jiān guò dé tài kuài le   dì yī cì zài zhōng guó guò shēng rì
杰明：感觉 时 间 过 得 太 快 了 ！**第 一 次** 在 中 国 过 生 日 ，
        yě gǎn jué hěn tè bié   hěn kāi xīn
        也 感 觉 很 **特别** 、很 **开心**！
Jamie: I feel **time flies really fast**! It's my **first time** to celebrate my birthday in China, it feels very **special** and **happy** too!

sū fēi duì le   lǐ lì yě huì lái   tā yǐ jīng wéi nǐ zuò le yī gè dà dàn gāo
苏飞：对 了 ，李 丽 也 来 ，她 **已 经** 为 你 做 了 一 个 **大蛋糕**。
Su Fei: By the way, Li Li will also come, she has **already** made a **big cake** for you.

jié míng zhēn de ma   wǒ dōu bù zhī dào tā huì zuò dàn gāo   tài lì hài le
杰明：真 的 吗？我 都 不 知 道 她 会 做 蛋 糕 ，太 **厉害** 了 ！
Jamie: Really? I didn't even know she could make cakes, so **amazing**!

sū fēi shì ā   tā bù jǐn huì zuò dàn gāo   hái huì zuò hěn duō qí tā měi shí
苏飞：是 啊！她 **不仅** 会 做 蛋 糕 ，**还 会** 做 很 多 其 他 美 食 。
Su Fei: Yes! **Not only** can she make cakes, **but also** many other delicacies.

jié míng qí shí   nǐ yě hěn lì hài   nǐ zuò de jiǎo zǐ zuì hǎo chī
杰明：其实 ，你 也 很 厉 害 ！你 做 的 **饺子** 最 好 吃 ！
Jamie: Actually, you are also very amazing! The **dumplings** you make taste the best!

sū fēi nǎ lǐ nǎ lǐ   duì le   hái yǒu shéi huì lái chī fàn
苏飞：哪 里 哪 里！对 了 ，**还有 谁** 会 来 吃 饭 ？
Su Fei: Thanks for the compliment! By the way, **who else** will come over for the meal?

杰明：还有我的美国朋友，我**已经**把饭店的**地址**发给他了。

Jamie: My American friend, I have **already** sent him the **address** of the restaurant.

苏飞：他**什么时候**到？

Su Fei: **When** will he arrive?

杰明：**可能**还有20**分钟**。

Jamie: **Possibly** another 20 minutes.

苏飞：李丽给我**发微信**了，说她10**分钟**后就**到**。

Su Fei: Li Li **sent** me a **WeChat message** and said she would **arrive** in 10 minutes.

杰明：那我们先**喝茶**吧，**慢慢**等他们。

Jamie: Well, let's **drink tea** first and **take our time** to wait for them.

苏飞：**好的**。

Su Fei: Okay.

Culture Corner

In China, it is traditionally not suitable to open gifts the moment you receive them. Although more and more young people are more open with the idea to open straight away. If you are not sure, just make sure you check with them beforehand!

Key Vocabulary

shēng rì 生 日	*n.*	birthday		lǐ wù 礼 物	*n.*	gift
dǎ kāi 打 开	*v.*	to open		jù huì 聚 会	*n.*	party
jié shù 结 束	*v.*	to end		gǎn jué 感 觉	*v.*	to feel
tè bié 特 别	*adj.*	special		kāi xīn 开 心	*adj.*	happy
dàn gāo 蛋 糕	*n.*	cake		lì hài 厉 害	*adj.*	amazing
fàn diàn 饭 店	*n.*	restaurant		dì zhǐ 地 址	*n.*	address

Chinese Version

苏飞：杰明，祝你生日快乐！

杰明：谢谢你！

苏飞：不客气！这是送给你的生日礼物。

杰明：哇！看上去真漂亮！我可以现在打开吗？

苏飞：唔，不可以！

杰明：为什么？

苏飞：因为在中国，我们收到礼物的时候，一般不可以马上打开。

杰明：那我什么时候才可以打开？

苏飞：等生日聚会结束以后，你才可以打开。

杰明：好吧。

苏飞：从今天开始，你就27岁了，感觉怎么样？

杰明：感觉时间过得太快了！第一次在中国过生日，也感觉很特别、
　　　很开心！

苏飞：对了，李丽也会来，她已经为你做了一个大蛋糕。

杰明：真的吗？我都不知道她会做蛋糕，太厉害了！

苏飞：是啊！她不仅会做蛋糕，还会做很多其他美食。

杰明：其实，你也很厉害！你做的饺子最好吃！

苏飞：哪里哪里！对了，还有谁会来吃饭？

杰明：还有我的美国朋友，我已经把饭店的地址发给他了。

苏飞：他什么时候到？

杰明：可能还有20分钟。

苏飞：李丽给我发微信了，说她10分钟后就到。

杰明：那我们先喝茶吧，慢慢等他们。

苏飞：好的。

25

租 房
zū　fáng

RENTING AN APARTMENT

gōng zuò rén yuán　xiān shēng　nín hǎo　qǐng jìn
工作人员：先生，您好！请进。
Staff:　　　Hello, **sir**! Please come in.

jié míng　　　xiè xie
杰明：　谢谢！
Jamie:　　　Thank you!

gōng zuò rén yuán　qǐng zuò　　qǐng wèn nín shì xiǎng mǎi fáng zǐ　　hái shì zū fáng zǐ
工作人员：请坐！请问您是想买房子，还是租房子？
Staff:　　　Please sit down. Would you like to **buy a place** or **rent a place**?

jié míng　　　wǒ xiǎng zū fáng zǐ
杰明：　我想租房子。
Jamie:　　　I would like to **rent a place**.

gōng zuò rén yuán　hǎo de　　qǐng wèn nín xiǎng zài nǎ lǐ zū
工作人员：好的，请问您想在哪里租？
Staff:　　　Okay, **where** do you want to rent?

jié míng　　　zài bǎo shān qū　　zuì hǎo hé dì tiě zhàn hěn jìn
杰明：　在宝山区，最好和地铁站很近。
Jamie:　　　In Baoshan **District**, it's best to be very close to the **subway station**.

gōng zuò rén yuán　kě yǐ　　nín xiǎng zū shén me yàng de fáng zǐ
工作人员：可以！您想租什么样的房子？
Staff:　　　Sure! **What kind of** apartment do you want to rent?

119

杰明： 是**套二**的房子，有一个**客厅**，两个**房间**。

Jamie: A **two-bedroom** apartment, with one **living room** and two **rooms**.

工作人员：好的。请问，还有其他**要求**吗？

Staff: Okay. Are there any other **requirements**?

杰明： 我还想要一个**厨房**和一个**洗手间**。

Jamie: I also want a **kitchen** and a **toilet**.

工作人员：**阳台**呢？

Staff: What about the **balcony**?

杰明： **如果**有阳台，**当然**更好。如果没有，也**没关系**！

Jamie: **If** there is a balcony, **of course** it would be better. If not, **it doesn't matter!**

工作人员：好的。请问，您的**价格**要求是？

Staff: Okay. May I ask, what's your **price** requirements?

杰明： 每个月在 3500 元**以下**。

Jamie: **Below** 3500 Yuan per month.

工作人员：好的！请问您想租**多长时间**？

Staff: Okay! **How long** would you like to rent for?

杰明： **可能**是一年。

Jamie: **Possibly** a year.

工作人员：好！请**等一下**，我去**查一查**。

Staff: Okay, please **wait a moment**, I will **have a check**.

五分钟后...

5 minutes later...

工作人员：先生，您看！这一套**怎么样**？它**符合**您的要

120

求，**而且**和**地铁站**只有 500 米。

Staff: Sir, look! **How about** this one? It **meets** your requirements, **plus** it is only 500 meters away from the **subway station**.

杰明：我**觉得**很好！**请问**，我可以去**看一看**吗？

Jamie: I think it's great! May I go to **have a look**?

工作人员：**当然可以**，您**什么时候****有时间**？我可以**带**您去。

Staff: Of course, when do you **have time**? I can **take** you there.

杰明：明天**中午** 12 点，**怎么样**？

Jamie: **How about** tomorrow at 12 **noon**?

工作人员：可以。**请问**您的**电话号码**是多少？

Staff: Yes. What is your **mobile number**?

杰明：是 19000060001

Jamie: It's 19000060001

工作人员：谢谢！明天我给您**打电话**。

Staff: Thank you! I will **call** you tomorrow.

Culture Corner

It's very common in China that the place to rent flats is also the place to buy flats. Rental prices are also higher in tier-1 cities like Beijing and Shanghai, and much lower in other cities.

Key Vocabulary

mǎi 买	*v.*	to buy	zū 租	*v.*	to rent
qū 区	*n.*	district	yāo qiú 要 求	*n.*	requirement
chú fáng 厨 房	*n.*	kitchen	xǐ shǒu jiān 洗 手 间	*n.*	washroom
yáng tái 阳 台	*n.*	balcony	kè tīng 客 厅	*n.*	living room
fáng jiān 房 间	*n.*	room	jià gé 价 格	*n.*	price
wò shì 卧 室	*n.*	bedroom	shū fáng 书 房	*n.*	study room
fáng zi 房 子	*n.*	house	gōng yù 公 寓	*n.*	apartment
yǐ xià 以 下	*n.*	below	kě néng 可 能	*adv.*	possibly
chá yī chá 查 一 查	*v.*	have a check	fú hé 符 合	*v.*	match/meet

Chinese Version

工作人员：先生，您好！请进。

杰明：谢谢！

工作人员：请坐！请问您是想买房子，还是租房子？

杰明：我想租房子。

工作人员：好的，请问您想在哪里租？

杰明：在宝山区，最好和地铁站很近。

工作人员：可以！您想租什么样的房子？

杰明：是套二的房子，有一个客厅，两个房间。

工作人员：好的。请问，还有其他要求吗？

杰明：我还想要一个厨房和一个洗手间。

工作人员：阳台呢？

杰明：如果有阳台，当然更好。如果没有，也没关系！

工作人员：好的。请问，您的价格要求是？

杰明：每个月在3500元以下。

工作人员：好的！请问您想租多长时间？

杰明：可能是一年。

工作人员：好！请等一下，我去查一查。

5 分钟后...

工作人员：先生，您看！这一套怎么样？它符合你的要求，而且和地
铁站只有500米。

杰明：我觉得很好！请问，我可以去看一看吗？

工作人员：当然可以，您什么时候有时间？我可以带你去。

杰明：明天中午12点，怎么样？

工作人员：可以。请问您的电话号码是多少？

杰明：是19000060001。

工作人员：谢谢！明天我给您打电话。

26

看 医 生
kàn yī shēng

SEEING A DOCTOR

jié míng nín hǎo qǐng wèn nín guì xìng
杰明：您好！请问您**贵姓**？

Jamie: Hello! What is your **surname**?

yī shēng wǒ xìng wáng nǐ kě yǐ jiào wǒ wáng yī shēng
医生：我姓王，你可以叫我王**医生**。

Doctor: My surname is Wang, you can call me **Doctor** Wang.

jié míng wáng yī shēng nín hǎo
杰明：王医生，您好！

Jamie: Hi, Doctor Wang!

yī shēng nín hǎo qǐng wèn nǐ nǎ lǐ bù shū fú
医生：您好！请问你哪里**不舒服**？

Doctor: Hello! May I ask, what is causing your **discomfort**?

jié míng wǒ zǒng shì jué dé hěn lèi bù jǐn tóu tòng ér qiě wǎn shàng yě shuì
杰明：我**总是**觉得很累，不仅**头痛**，而且晚上也**睡**
bù hǎo
不好。

Jamie: I **always** feel very tired. Not only do I have a **headache**, but I **can't sleep
well** at night.

yī shēng nǐ shì cóng shén me shí hòu kāi shǐ bù shū fú de
医生：你是从**什么时候**开始不舒服的？

Doctor: **When** did you start to feel sick?

jié míng cóng sān tiān qián
杰明：从 三 天 **前** 。
Jamie: From three days **ago**.

yī shēng kě néng fā shāo le　　qǐngyòng zhè gè cè yī xià nǐ de tǐ wēn
医生：可能 **发烧** 了，请用 这 个 **测 一 下** 你 的 **体温** 。
Doctor: Maybe you **have a fever**. Please **have a check of** your **body temperature** with this.

jié míng hǎo de
杰明：好 的 。
Jamie: Okay.

liǎng fēn zhōng hòu
两 分 钟 后 …
2 minutes later

yī shēng wǒ kàn kàn　shì　dù　zhēn de fā shāo le　nǐ ké sòu ma
医生：我 看 看，是 39 度，真 的 发烧 了 。你 **咳嗽** 吗？
Doctor: Let me see, it is 39 degrees. You do have a fever. Do you **cough**?

jié míng duì　dàn zhǐ shì zǎo shàng ké sòu
杰明：对，但 **只是** 早 上 咳嗽 。
Jamie: Yes, but **only** coughing in the morning.

yī shēng hái yǒu nǎ lǐ bù shū fú ma
医生：还 有 哪里 不 舒服 吗？
Doctor: Is there any other issue (where discomfort)?

jié míng bí zǐ yě bù shū fú　yǒu shí hòu hái liú bí tì
杰明：**鼻子** 也 不 舒服，有 时候 还 **流 鼻 涕** 。
Jamie: My **nose** is also uncomfortable, sometimes I have a **runny nose**.

yī shēng nǐ zhè xiē tiān chī dé zěn me yàng
医生：你 这 些 天 吃 得 **怎么样**？
Doctor: **How** are you eating these days?

jié míng qí shí　zhè xiē tiān dōu bù tài xiǎng chī dōng xī　suǒ yǐ　chī dé bù duō
杰明：其实，**这 些 天** 都 不 太 想 吃 东 西，**所以**，吃 得 不 多 。
Jamie: Actually, I don't feel like eating **these days**, **so** I don't eat much.

yī shēng nǐ shì dé gǎn mào le　zhè shì yào dān zǐ
医生：你 是 **得 感冒** 了，这 是 **药 单 子** 。
Doctor: You **have a cold**. Here is the **medicine list**.

jié míng xiè xie
杰明：谢谢 ！
Jamie: Thank you!

医生：你要按时**吃药**，还要**多休息**，多喝水。一个星期
后，应该会好。如果不好，请**再来**。

Doctor: You need to **take medicine** on time, **rest more** and drink plenty of water. After a week, it should be better. If not, please **come again**.

杰明：好的。请问在哪里拿药？

Jamie: Okay. Where can I **get the medicine?**

医生：在二楼的 202 **药房**。

Doctor: In **pharmacy room** 202 on the second floor.

杰明：谢谢你，再见。

Jamie: Thank you, goodbye.

医生：再见！

Doctor: Goodbye!

Culture Corner

In many Western countries, otherwise healthy people do not tend to see a doctor for a cold, however this is very common in China. Your health is important, especially when traveling or living abroad; read and listen carefully to pick up some useful words and phrases in case you ever need to see the doctor in China.

Key Vocabulary

guì xìng 贵 姓	n.	surname (respectful)	yī shēng 医 生	n.	doctor
lèi 累	adj.	tired	tóu tòng 头 痛	adj.	headache
kāi shǐ 开 始	v.	start	cóng 从	v.	from
fā shāo 发 烧	v.	have a fever	tǐ wēn 体 温	n.	body temperature
ké sòu 咳 嗽	v. n.	to cough cough	bí zǐ 鼻 子	n.	nose
liú bí tì 流 鼻 涕	v.	to have runny nose	gǎn mào 感 冒	n.	cold
yào dān zǐ 药 单 子	n.	medicine list	chī yào 吃 药	v.	take medicine

Supplementary Vocabulary

shì gù 事 故	n.	accident	fù xiè 腹 泻	n.	diarrhoea
jiù hù chē 救 护 车	n.	ambulance	wèi tòng 胃 痛	n.	stomach ache
jí zhěn shì 急 诊 室	n.	emergency room	gē shāng 割 伤	n.	cut
jìng luán 痉 挛	n.	cramp	cā shāng 擦 伤	n.	graze
xiào chuǎn 哮 喘	n.	asthma	yū shāng 瘀 伤	n.	bruise
pí zhěn 皮 疹	n.	rash	shāo shāng 烧 伤	n.	burn
bí xuè 鼻 血	n.	nosebleed	yǎo shāng 咬 伤	n.	bite
ě xīn 恶 心	n.	nausea	zhé shāng 蛰 伤	n.	sting
liú gǎn 流 感	n.	flu	niǔ shāng 扭 伤	n.	sprain

127

Chinese Version

杰明：您好！请问您贵姓？

医生：我姓王，你可以叫我王医生。

杰明：王医生，您好！

医生：您好！请问你哪里不舒服？

杰明：我总是觉得很累，不仅头痛，而且晚上也睡不好。

医生：你是从什么时候开始不舒服的？

杰明：从三天前。

医生：可能发烧了，请用这个测一下你的体温。

杰明：好的。

2 分钟后⋯

医生：我看看，是39度，真的发烧了。你咳嗽吗？

杰明：对，但只是早上咳嗽。

医生：还有哪里不舒服吗？

杰明：鼻子也不舒服，有时候还流鼻涕。

医生：你这些天吃得怎么样？

杰明：其实，这些天都不太想吃东西，所以，吃得不多。

医生：你是得感冒了，这是药单子。

杰明：谢谢！

医生：你要按时吃药，还要多休息，多喝水。一个星期后，应该会好。
如果不好，请再来。

杰明：好的。请问在哪里拿药？

医生：在二楼的202药房。

杰明：谢谢你，再见。

医生：再见！

27

圣诞快乐！
shèng dàn kuài lè

MERRY CHRISTMAS!

苏飞：杰明，你在看什么？
sū fēi jié míng nǐ zài kàn shén me

Su Fei: Jamie, what are you looking at?

杰明：在手机上看**新闻**。哇！你今天**看上去**真漂亮！
jié míng zài shǒu jī shàng kàn xīn wén wā nǐ jīn tiān kàn shàng qù zhēn piào liàng

Jamie: Just **news** on the phone. Wow! You **look** so beautiful today!

苏飞：你知道今天是什么**日子**吗？
sū fēi nǐ zhī dào jīn tiān shì shén me rì zǐ ma

Su Fei: Do you know what **day** is today?

杰明：大家都知道！今天是**圣诞节**！
jié míng dà jiā dōu zhī dào jīn tiān shì shèng dàn jié

Jamie: Everyone knows! Today is **Christmas**!

苏飞：对！我**以为**你忘了！祝你**圣诞快乐**！
sū fēi duì wǒ yǐ wéi nǐ wàng le zhù nǐ shèng dàn kuài lè

Su Fei: Yes! I **thought** you forgot! Wish you **Merry Christmas**!

杰明：怎么可能**忘**！圣诞快乐！你看，这是给你的**礼物**。
jié míng zěn me kě néng wàng shèng dàn kuài lè nǐ kàn zhè shì gěi nǐ de lǐ wù

Jamie: How could I **forget**! Merry Christmas! You see, this is a **gift** for you.

苏飞：我可以**打开**看看吗？
sū fēi wǒ kě yǐ dǎ kāi kàn kàn ma

Su Fei: Can I **open** it to have a look?

jié míng dāng rán kě yǐ
杰明：当然可以。

Jamie: Of course.

sū fēi wā shì xuě rén qiú zhēn shì tài měi le xiè xie nǐ
苏飞：哇！是雪人球！真是太美了！谢谢你！

Su Fei: Wow! It's a **snowman glass ball**! So beautiful! Thank you!

jié míng bù kè qì wǒ zhī dào nǐ zuì xǐ huān kàn xià xuě xiàn zài kě yǐ tiān tiān
杰明：不客气，我知道你最喜欢看下雪，现在可以天天
kàn lā
看啦。

Jamie: You're welcome, I know you like watching **snowing** the most, now you can watch it **every day**.

sū fēi tài bàng le zhè shì wǒ sòng gěi nǐ de lǐ wù nǐ dǎ kāi kàn kàn
苏飞：太棒了！这是我送给你的礼物，你打开看看。

Su Fei: Great! This is my **gift** to you. Open and **take a look**.

jié míng xiè xie ā shì yī jiàn lán sè de chènshān wǒ hěn xǐ huān duì le
杰明：谢谢！啊，是一件蓝色的衬衫，我很喜欢！对了，
nǐ zhī dào ma zuó tiān wǒ shōu dào le hěn duō píng guǒ
你知道吗？昨天我收到了很多苹果。

Jamie: Thank you! Ah, it's a blue **shirt**, I love it! By the way, do you know? I **received** many apples yesterday.

sū fēi shì nǐ de tóng xué sòng gěi nǐ de ma
苏飞：是你的同学送给你的吗？

Su Fei: Did your **classmates** give them to you?

jié míng shì ā tā men shuō zài píng ān yè yìng gāi chī píng guǒ
杰明：是啊！他们说在平安夜应该吃苹果。

Jamie: Yes! They said everyone should eat apples on **Christmas Eve**.

sū fēi duì zài píng ān yè zhōng guó rén xǐ huān sòng píng guǒ chī píng guǒ
苏飞：对，在平安夜，中国人喜欢送苹果、吃苹果。

Su Fei: Yes, on Christmas Eve, we like to **give away apples** and eat apples in China.

jié míng wèi shén me
杰明：为什么？

Jamie: Why?

sū fēi yīn wèi píng ān de píng hé píng guǒ de píng tóng
苏飞：因为"平安"的"平"和"苹果"的"苹"同
yīn chī píng guǒ shì píng ān de yì sī
音。吃苹果是平安的意思。

Su Fei: Because the Chinese character "píng" from the word "apple" **sounds the same** as another "píng" from the word of "peace". Eating apples means having **peace**.

杰明：这真**有趣**！你呢，**昨天**吃苹果了吗？

jié míng zhè zhēn yǒu qù   nǐ ne   zuó tiān chī píng guǒ le ma

Jamie: This is so **fun**! What about you, did you eat apples **yesterday**?

苏飞：吃了，是公司**同事**送的。

sū fēi   chī le   shì gōng sī tóng shì sòng de

Su Fei: I did. They were given by company **colleagues**.

杰明：我和同学们**今天晚上**去**歌厅**唱歌，你想去吗？

jié míng wǒ hé tóng xué men jīn tiān wǎn shàng qù gē tīng chàng gē   nǐ xiǎng qù ma

Jamie: My classmates and I will go to the **karaoke** to sing **tonight**. Do you want to come with us?

苏飞：好啊！什么时候去？

sū fēi   hǎo ā   shén me shí hòu qù

Su Fei: Alright! What time?

杰明：晚上7点。

jié míng wǎn shàng diǎn

Jamie: 7 o'clock in the evening.

苏飞：好！

sū fēi   hǎo

Su Fei: OK!

Culture Corner

Although Christmas is not a public holiday in China, many companies and individuals celebrate it. Giving apples as gifts is a tradition on Christmas Eve as the apple represents peace due to the words sounding similar in Chinese. Hence, apples are also called the fruit of peace on this day.

píngguǒ	píng ān	píng ān guǒ
苹果	平安	平安果
apple	peace	peace fruit

Key Vocabulary

xīn wén 新 闻	*n.*	news	kàn shàng qù 看 上 去		look like	
rì zǐ 日 子	*n.*	date / day	shèng dàn jié 圣 诞 节	*n.*	Christmas festival	
shèng dàn kuài lè 圣 诞 快 乐		Merry Christmas	wàng 忘	*v.*	to forget	
píng ān yè 平 安 夜	*n.*	Christmas Eve	píng ān 平 安	*n.*	peace	
tóng xué 同 学	*n.*	classmate	tóng shì 同 事	*n.*	colleague	
yǒu qù 有 趣	*adj.*	interesting	gē tīng 歌 厅	*n.*	karaoke	
shèng dàn lǎo rén 圣 诞 老 人	*n.*	Father Christmas	shèng dàn shù 圣 诞 树	*n.*	Christmas tree	

Chinese Version

苏 飞：杰明，你在看什么？

杰 明：在手机上看新闻。哇！你今天看上去真漂亮！

苏 飞：你知道今天是什么日子吗？

杰 明：大家都知道！今天是圣诞节！

苏 飞：对！我以为你忘了！祝你圣诞快乐！

杰 明：怎么可能忘！圣诞快乐！你看，这是给你的礼物。

苏 飞：我可以打开看看吗？

杰 明：当然可以。

苏 飞：哇！是雪人球！真是太美了！谢谢你！

杰 明：不客气，我知道你最喜欢看下雪，现在可以天天看啦。

苏 飞：太棒了！这是我送给你的礼物，你打开看看。

杰 明：谢谢！啊，是一件蓝色的衬衫，我很喜欢！对了，你知道吗？昨天我收到了很多苹果。

苏 飞：是你的同学送给你的吗？

杰 明：是啊！他们说在平安夜应该吃苹果。

苏 飞：对，在平安夜，中国人喜欢送苹果、吃苹果。

杰 明：为什么？

苏 飞：因为"平安"的"平"和"苹果"的"苹"同音。吃苹果是平安的意思。

杰 明：这真有趣！你呢，昨天吃苹果了吗？

苏 飞：吃了，是公司同事送的。

杰 明：我和同学们今天晚上去歌厅唱歌，你想去吗？

苏 飞：好啊！什么时候去？

杰 明：晚上7点。

苏 飞：好！

28 用微信还是支付宝？
yòng wēi xìn hái shì zhī fù bǎo

WECHAT OR ALIPAY?

sū fēi nǐ yǐ jīng lái zhōng guó bàn nián le gǎn jué zěn me yàng
苏飞: 你**已经**来中国**半年**了，**感觉**怎么样？
Su Fei: You **have been** in China for **half a year**, what do you **feel**?

jié míng jué dé hěn kāi xīn zài zhōng guó shēng huó tài fāng biàn le
杰明: 觉得很**开心**，在中国生活太**方便**了！
Jamie: I feel very **happy**, living in China is so **convenient**!

sū fēi nǎ lǐ fāng biàn shì gōng gòng jiāo tōng hái shì chī hē zhù xíng
苏飞: 哪里方便？是**公共交通**，还是**吃喝住行**？
Su Fei: What (aspect) is convenient? Is it **public transportation**, or **basic necessities** (food, drink, accommodation and transportation)?

jié míng zhè xiē dōu hěn fāng biàn yīn wèi dōu kě yǐ yòng shǒu jī wán chéng
杰明: 这些**都**很方便，因为都可以用手机**完成**。
Jamie: These are **all** convenient because they can all be **completed** with a mobile phone.

sū fēi wǒ zuì xǐ huān zài wǎng shàng mǎi dōng xī dōng xī duō xuǎn zé yě duō
苏飞: 我最喜欢在**网上**买东西，**东西**多，**选择**也多！
Su Fei: I like shopping **online** the most. There are lots of **things** and so many **choices**!

jié míng ér qiě wǒ yǐ jīng xí guàn le zài wǎng shàng diǎn cān dǎ chē dìng
杰明: 而且，我已经**习惯**了在网上**点餐**、打车、订
jiǔ diàn
酒店。

134

Jamie: Besides, I'm also **used to ordering food**, taxis, and hotels online.

苏飞：是 啊！我 记 得 你 也 下 载 了 打 车 的 **手 机 程 序**，对 吗？

Su Fei: Indeed! I **remember** you already downloaded the taxi **mobile app**, right?

杰明：对！这 个 真 的 非 常 **好 用**，我 最 喜 欢！虽 然，我 常 常 坐 地 铁 **出 门**。但 是，有 时 候 也 喜 欢 **打 车**，又 方 便、又 便 宜。

Jamie: Yes! This is really **useful**, my favourite! Although, I usually take the subway to **go out**. However, sometimes I like to **take a taxi**, and this app makes it convenient and cheap.

苏飞：其 实，在 英 国 的 时 候，**也** 可 以 在 **网 上** 做 很 多 事。

Su Fei: Actually, when you were in the UK, you can **also** do a lot of things **online**.

杰明：没 错！**可 是**，在 中 国，可 以 在 **网 上** 做 的 事 更 多、更 快、更 方 便。

Jamie: That's right! **However**, in China, you can do more **online**, and it's faster, and more convenient.

苏飞：那 你 觉 得 **微 信** 怎 么 样！

Su Fei: What do you think of **WeChat**?

杰明：我 已 经 **离 不 开** 微 信 了！**因 为**，打 电 话、**发 短 信**、买 东 西 都 用 微 信。

Jamie: I already **can't live without** WeChat! **Because** I need it for making calls, **sending text messages**, and paying for things.

苏飞：我 也 是！**每 次** 付 钱，**要 么** 用 微 信，**要 么** 用 支 付 宝。

Su Fei: Me too! **Every time** I pay, **either** by WeChat, **or** by Alipay.

杰明：对 啊！我 **发 现**，现 在 很 多 商 店 都 不 收 **现 金**。

Jamie: Indeed! I **notice** that many stores now do not accept **cash**.

苏飞：对！现在的中国**差不多**是个**无现金社会**，大家**主要**用微信，或支付宝付钱。

Su Fei: Yes! China is **almost** a **cashless society** nowadays. People **mainly** pay by WeChat or Alipay.

杰明：微信和支付宝，哪个用得**更多**？

Jamie: WeChat or Alipay, which one is **more** used?

苏飞：我觉得是**微信**。**比如说**，我只用**支付宝**在网上买东西。

Su Fei: I think it's **WeChat**. **For example**, I only use **Alipay** to buy things online.

杰明：在**公司**，大家也用微信吗？

Jamie: In **companies**, do people also use WeChat?

苏飞：是的，我的公司有**微信群**，同事们经常在群里**发消息**。

Su Fei: Yes, my company has a **WeChat group**, and colleagues often **send messages** in the group.

杰明：我们学校的**老师**和**同学**也用微信群**发通知**。

Jamie: Teachers and **classmates** in our university also **send notifications** in our WeChat group.

Key Vocabulary

wēi xìn 微信	n	WeChat		zhī fù bǎo 支付宝	n	Alipay
gōnggòng jiāo tōng 公共交通	n.	public transport		qún 群	n.	group
wán chéng 完成	v.	to complete		diǎn cān 点餐	vp.	to order food
dǎ chē 打车	vp.	take taxi		dìng jiǔ diàn 订酒店	vp.	to book a hotel
hǎo yòng 好用	adj.	useful		lí bù kāi 离不开	vp.	cannot live without
duǎn xìn 短信	n.	text message		xiàn jīn 现金	n.	cash
bǐ rú shuō 比如说		for example		gōng sī 公司	n.	company
chī hē zhù xíng 吃喝住行		daily necessities (eat, drink, live, travel)		tōng zhī 通知	n.	notification

Culture Corner

China has come from being a cash-based society to almost cashless with ubiquitous mobile payments. Apps such as WeChat and Alipay see over 1 trillion RMB in transactions a year.

There are mobile apps covering many aspects of daily life in China, from shopping to travel, and much more.

Chinese Version

苏 飞：你已经来中国半年了，感觉怎么样？

杰 明：觉得很开心，在中国生活太方便了！

苏 飞：哪里方便？是公共交通，还是吃喝住行？

杰 明：这些都很方便，因为都可以用手机完成。

苏 飞：我最喜欢在网上买东西，东西多，选择也多！

杰 明：而且，我已经习惯了在网上点餐、打车、订酒店。

苏 飞：是啊！我记得你也下载了打车的手机程序，对吗？

杰 明：对！这个真的非常好用，我最喜欢！虽然，我常常坐地铁出门。但是，有时候也喜欢打车，又方便、又便宜。

苏 飞：其实，在英国的时候，也可以在网上做很多事。

杰 明：没错！可是，在中国，可以在网上做的事更多、更快、更方便。

苏 飞：那你觉得微信怎么样！

杰 明：我已经离不开微信了！因为，打电话、发短信、买东西都用微信。

苏 飞：我也是！每次付钱，要么用微信，要么用支付宝。

杰 明：对啊！我发现，现在很多商店都不收现金。

苏 飞：对！现在的中国差不多是个无现金社会，大家主要用微信，或支付宝付钱。

杰 明：微信和支付宝，哪个用得更多？

苏 飞：我觉得是微信。比如说，我只用支付宝在网上买东西。

杰 明：在公司，大家也用微信吗？

苏 飞：是的，我的公司有微信群，同事们经常在群里发消息。

杰 明：我们学校的老师和同学也用微信群发通知。

29

找 工 作
zhǎo gōng zuò

FINDING A JOB

杰明：飞飞，我想**告诉**你**一件事**。
jié míng fēi fēi wǒ xiǎng gào sù nǐ yī jiàn shì

Jamie: Feifei, I want to **tell** you something(**one matter**).

苏飞：是什么事？
sū fēi shì shén me shì

Su Fei: What is it?

杰明：我在学校里的学习已经**结束**了，现在我**打算**找工作。
jié míng wǒ zài xué xiào lǐ de xué xí yǐ jīng jié shù le xiàn zài wǒ dǎ suàn zhǎo gōng zuò

Jamie: My studies in the university are already **over**, and now I **plan to** find a job.

苏飞：太好了，我**支持**你！
sū fēi tài hǎo le wǒ zhī chí nǐ

Su Fei: That's great, I **support** you!

杰明：谢谢你！我知道不**容易**，但我**一定**要试一试。
jié míng xiè xie nǐ wǒ zhī dào bù róng yì dàn wǒ yī dìng yào shì yī shì

Jamie: Thank you! I know it is not **easy**, but I **must** have a try.

苏飞：你想找**什么样**的工作？
sū fēi nǐ xiǎng zhǎo shén me yàng de gōng zuò

Su Fei: **What kind of** job are you looking for?

杰明：还不知道，**但是**已经有两家公司**联系**我了。
jié míng hái bù zhī dào dàn shì yǐ jīng yǒu liǎng jiā gōng sī lián xì wǒ le

139

Jamie: I don't know yet, **but** two companies have **contacted** me.

苏飞：是两家什么**公司**？

sū fēi　shì liǎng jiā shén me gōng sī

Su Fei: Which two **companies**?

杰明：是一家中国的**教育**公司，和一家美国的**进出口**公司，都在上海。

jié míng　shì yī jiā zhōng guó de jiào yù gōng sī　hé yī jiā měi guó de jìn chū kǒu gōng sī　dōu zài shàng hǎi

Jamie: It's a Chinese **education** company and an American **import and export** company, both in Shanghai.

苏飞：是什么工作？

sū fēi　shì shén me gōng zuò

Su Fei: What are the job roles?

杰明：第一个是**英语老师**，第二个是**业务经理**。

jié míng　dì yī gè shì yīng yǔ lǎo shī　dì èr gè shì yè wù jīng lǐ

Jamie: The first one is an **English teacher** position, and the second is a **business manager** position.

苏飞：**工资**怎么样？

sū fēi　gōng zī zěn me yàng

Su Fei: How are the **salaries**?

杰明：第一个是**每月**二万元，第二个，我还不知道。

jié míng　dì yī gè shì měi yuè èr wàn yuán　dì èr gè　wǒ hái bù zhī dào

Jamie: The first one is 20,000 Yuan **per month**, as for the second one, I don't know yet.

苏飞：你觉得自己**更喜欢**哪个？

sū fēi　nǐ jué dé zì jǐ gèng xǐ huān nǎ gè

Su Fei: Which one do you **like more**?

杰明：不知道，我要好好**想一想**。

jié míng　bù zhī dào　wǒ yào hǎo hǎo xiǎng yī xiǎng

Jamie: I don't know, I have to **think about it**.

苏飞：这两家公司都可以**帮助**你办**工作签证**吗？

sū fēi　zhè liǎng jiā gōng sī dōu kě yǐ bāng zhù nǐ bàn gōng zuò qiān zhèng ma

Su Fei: Can both companies **help** you apply for a **work visa**?

杰明：是的。

jié míng　shì de

Jamie: Yes.

苏飞：太好了！有了工作签，你就可以在中国**长住**了。

sū fēi　tài hǎo le　yǒu le gōng zuò qiān　nǐ jiù kě yǐ zài zhōng guó cháng zhù le

Su Fei: That's great! With a work visa, you can **stay longer** in China.

杰明：jié míng shì ā wǒ hěn xǐ huān zài zhōng guó shēng huó rú guǒ néng yī biān gōng
杰明：是 啊！我 很 喜 欢 在 中 国 **生 活**。如 果 能 **一 边 工**
zuò yī biān shēng huó dāng rán gèng hǎo
作，**一 边 生 活**，当 然 更 好！

Jamie: Yes! I enjoy **living** in China very much. And of course it would be better if I could **enjoy life while working**!

sū fēi wǒ tóng yì duì le nǐ shén me shí hòu miàn shì
苏飞：我 **同 意**！对 了，你 什 么 时 候 **面 试**？

Su Fei: I **agree**! By the way, when are your **interviews**?

jié míng dì yī gè shì xīng qī wǔ dì èr gè shì liǎng gè xīng qī hòu
杰明：**第 一 个** 是 星 期 五，**第 二 个** 是 两 个 星 期 后。

Jamie: **The first one** is on Friday, and **the second one** is in two weeks' time.

sū fēi jiā yóu wǒ xiāng xìn nǐ yī dìng huì chénggōng
苏飞：加 油，我 **相 信** 你 一 定 会 **成 功**！

Su Fei: Come on! I **believe** you will **succeed**!

jié míng xiè xie nǐ
杰明：谢 谢 你！

Jamie: Thank you!

Learning Tip

yī biān
一 边 is used to connect two actions (verbs or verbal phrases) to indicate two things happening at the same time:

yī biān yī biān
一边 + Verb1 + 一边 + Verb2

Key Vocabulary

gào sù 告诉	*v.*	to tell	jié shù 结束	*v.*	to end
zhǎogōng zuò 找工作	*vp.*	to find a job	zhī chí 支持	*v.*	to support
róng yì 容易	*adj.*	easy	shì yī shì 试一试	*vp.*	have a try
lián xì 联系	*v.*	to contact	jiào yù 教育	*n.*	education
jìn kǒu 进口	*v.*	to import	chū kǒu 出口	*v.*	to export
lǎo shī 老师	*n.*	teacher	jīng lǐ 经理	*n.*	manager
gōng zī 工资	*n.*	salary	gōng zuò 工作	*v.*	to work
qiān zhèng 签证	*n.*	visa	tóng yì 同意	*v.*	to agree
miàn shì 面试	*n.* *v.*	interview to have interview	chéng gōng 成功	*adj.* *v.*	successful to succeed

Chinese Version

杰明：飞飞，我想告诉你一件事。

苏飞：是什么事？

杰明：我在学校里的学习已经结束了，现在我打算找工作。

苏飞：太好了，我支持你！

杰明：谢谢你！我知道不容易，但我一定要试一试。

苏飞：你想找什么样的工作？

杰明：还不知道，但是已经有两家公司联系我了。

苏飞：是两家什么公司？

杰明：是一家中国的教育公司，和一家美国的进出口公司，都在上海。

苏飞：是什么工作？

杰明：第一个是英语老师，第二个是业务经理。

苏飞：工资怎么样？

杰明：第一个是每月二万元，第二个，我还不知道。

苏飞：你觉得自己更喜欢哪个？

杰明：不知道，我要好好想一想。

苏飞：这两家公司都可以帮助你办工作签证吗？

杰明：是的。

苏飞：太好了！有了工作签，你就可以在中国长住了。

杰明：是啊！我很喜欢在中国生活。如果能一边工作，一边生活，当然更好！

苏飞：我同意！对了，你什么时候面试？

杰明：第一个是星期五，第二个是两个星期后。

苏飞：加油，我相信你一定会成功！

杰明：谢谢你！

30 新年快乐！
xīn nián kuài lè

HAPPY NEW YEAR!

jié míng　xīn nián kuài lè
杰明：新年 快乐！

Jamie:　Happy **New Year**!

sū fēi　xīn nián kuài lè　zhù nǐ shēn tǐ jiàn kāng　wàn shì rú yì
苏飞：新年 快乐！祝你**身体健康**，**万事如意**！

Su Fei:　Happy New Year! I wish you **good health** and that **everything goes well**!

jié míng　xiè xie nǐ　shí jiān guò dé zhēn kuài ā
杰明：谢谢你！**时间** 过 得 真 快 啊！

Jamie:　Thank you! **Time** flies so fast!

sū fēi　shì ā　qù nián wǒ men zài yīng guó guò xīn nián　jīn nián zài zhōng guó guò
苏飞：是 啊！**去年** 我们 在 英国 **过新年**，**今年** 在 中 国 过
xīn nián
新 年。

Su Fei:　Indeed! We **celebrated the New Year** in the UK **last year** and **this year** in
　　　　China.

jié míng　wǒ hěn gāo xīng zhè gè xīng qī nǐ bù shàng bān　kě yǐ hǎo hǎo xiū xī
杰明：我 很 高兴 这 个 星 期 你 不 **上班**，可以 **好好休息**、
hǎo hǎo guò nián
好好过年！

Jamie:　I'm very happy that you're not **working** this week, so you can **have a**
　　　　good rest and **enjoy a great new year**!

sū fēi　ng　zhōng guó xīn nián yě shì zhōng guó de chūn jié　jīn tiān　wǒ men guò
苏飞：嗯，中 国 新 年 也 是 中 国 的 **春节**！今天，我 们 过

xīn nián　　yě guò chūn jié
新 年 、也 过 春 节！

Su Fei: Well, Chinese New Year is also **Chinese Spring Festival**! Today, we celebrate the New Year and the Spring Festival together!

jié míng　duì　　zhù wǒ men chūn jié kuài lè
杰明：对！祝 我 们 **春 节 快 乐**！

Jamie: True! **Happy Spring Festival**!

sū fēi　　nǐ kàn　　wǒ jīn tiān zuò le　yī tiáo　　hóng shāo yú
苏飞：你 看，我 今 天 **做** 了 一 条 "红 烧 鱼"。

Su Fei: Look, I **made** a "red braised fish" today.

jié míng　hǎo xiāng ā　　duì le　　wèi shén me jīn tiān yào chī yú
杰明：好 香 啊！对 了，**为 什 么** 今 天 要 吃 鱼？

Jamie: It smells so good! By the way, **why** do we eat fish today?

sū fēi　　nǐ méi tīng guò ma　　　　nián nián yǒu yú
苏飞：你 没 听 过 吗 ——"年 年 有 余"？

Su Fei: Haven't you heard of the idiom - "have surplus each year"?

jié míng　　nián nián yǒu yú　　shì shén me yì sī
杰明："年 年 有 余" 是 什 么 意 思？

Jamie: What does this mean?

sū fēi　　yì sī shì měi nián dōu yǒu　shèng yú　　　　yīn wèi　yú　hé　yú　tóng
苏飞：**意 思** 是 每 年 都 有 "剩 余"。**因 为** "余" 和 "鱼" 同
yīn　suǒ yǐ chī yú shì　shēng huó hǎo　　yǒu　shèng yú
音，所 以 吃 鱼 是：生 活 好，有 "剩 余"。

Su Fei: **It means** there is "surplus" for every year. **Because** the Chinese character for "surplus" **sounds the same** as the word "fish", so eating fish means: good life with enough "surplus".

jié míng zhēn yǒu qù　　nà wǒ yě zhù nǐ　　nián nián yǒu yú
杰明：真 **有 趣**！那 我 也 **祝 你** "年 年 有 余"！

Jamie: That's **interesting**! Then I also **wish you** "have surplus each year!"

sū fēi　　duì le　　wǒ zhǔn bèi de hóng bāo zài nǎ ér
苏飞：对 了，我 准 备 的 **红 包** 在 哪 儿？

Su Fei: Hmm, where are the **red packets** I prepared?

jié míng　zài diàn nǎo páng biān　míng tiān nǐ de bà mā huì lái　　zhè hóng bāo shì gěi
杰明：在 **电 脑** 旁 边，明 天 你 的 爸 妈 会 来，这 **红 包** 是 给
tā men de ma
他 们 的 吗？

Jamie: Next to the **computer**, your parents will come tomorrow. Are these red **packets** for them?

苏飞：是啊！**我小的时候**，爸妈给我红包。现在，是我
给他们红包。

Su Fei: Yes! **When I was little**, my parents gave me red packets. Now, it's my turn

to give them red packets.

Culture Corner

Chinese New Year falls on the first date of the first month in the Lunar Calendar, it also marks the start of the Spring season, that's why it is also called Spring Festival. Sending good wishes, eating fish, giving red packets (contains money) are part of the traditional activities.

Key Vocabulary

新年 xīn nián	*n.*	New Year	快乐 kuài lè	*adj.*	happy
今年 jīn nián	*n.*	this year	去年 qù nián	*n.*	last year
明年 míng nián	*n.*	next year	生活 shēng huó	*n.*	life
身体健康 shēn tǐ jiàn kāng	*idiom*	good health	时间 shí jiān	*n.*	time
万事如意 wàn shì rú yì	*idiom*	everything goes well	春节 chūn jié	*n.*	Spring Festival
过(新)年 guò xīn nián	*vp.*	celebrate new year	红包 hóng bāo	*n.*	red packet
年年有余 nián nián yǒu yú	*idiom*	have surplus every year	电脑 diàn nǎo	*n.*	computer

Chinese Version

杰明：新年快乐！

苏飞：新年快乐！祝你身体健康，万事如意！

杰明：谢谢你！时间过得真快啊！

苏飞：是啊！去年我们在英国过新年，今年在中国过新年。

杰明：我很高兴这个星期你不上班，可以好好休息、好好过年！

苏飞：嗯，中国新年也是中国的春节！今天，我们过新年、也过春节！

杰明：对！祝我们春节快乐！

苏飞：你看，我今天做了一条"红烧鱼"。

杰明：好香啊！对了，为什么今天要吃鱼?。

苏飞：你没听过吗——"年年有余"？

杰明："年年有余"是什么意思？

苏飞：意思是每年都有"剩余"。因为"余"和"鱼"同音，所以吃鱼是：
　　　生活好，有"剩余"。

杰明：真有趣！那我也祝你"年年有余"！

苏飞：对了，我准备的红包在哪儿？

杰明：在电脑旁边，明天你的爸妈会来，这红包是给他们的吗？

苏飞：是啊！我小的时候，爸妈给我红包。现在，是我给他们红包。

ACCESS AUDIO

I highly encourage you to use the accompanying audio recordings for all of the conversations in this book, not only will it help to improve your listening skills but if you are unfamiliar or unsure about the pronunciations of any words in this book, then you can listen to them spoken by native speakers.

INSTRUCTIONS TO ACCESS AUDIO

1.   Scan the QR code on this page

                 or
                Go to:
www.linglingmandarin.com/books

2.   Locate this book in the list

3.   Click the "Access Audio" button

                                      Access Audio

4.   Enter the password (case-sensitive):

                                     Please enter the password below.

5fQhsjA

                                     Password

5.   Select your preferred option to listen
         to the audio

THE NEXT STAGE

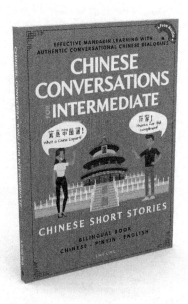

Congratulations on reaching the end of this book! By now, you're well on your way to progressing to the intermediate level. It is my pleasure to welcome you to the next stage and encourage you to continue your journey with my second book of my Spoken Chinese series: **Chinese Conversations for Intermediate**!

This book focuses on language foundation building and resolving daily tasks, whereas the intermediate edition is upgraded and more expansive in all aspects. It consists of twice as many expanded dialogues, covering contemporary hot topics, lifestyle, Chinese culture and traditions, and funny stories that will make you smile and remember all while having fun! You will expand your daily vocabulary and learn fun Chinese slang and witty idiomatic phrases that will make you stand out from the crowd. The book will also immerse you in authentic Chinese spoken language, including casual and friendly conversations, business talk, romantic talk, and even the odd joke or two. Moreover, you will learn deeply about modern and traditional Chinese festivals, such as Chinese Single's Day, Chinese New Year, Moon Festival, and more.

Thank you again, dearest readers. May you enjoy a happy and abundant Mandarin learning journey, I look forward to being with you again in your next stage learning.

Available now:
https://amzn.to/3Z3xwHU

GET YOUR
FREE
EBOOK NOW

linglingmandarin.com/beginner-bundle

CHINESE
CONVERSATIONS
FOR BEGINNERS

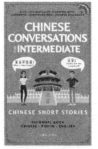
CHINESE
CONVERSATIONS
FOR INTERMEDIATE

LEARN CHINESE
VOCABULARY
FOR BEGINNERS
(NEW HSK 1)

CHINESE STORIES
FOR LANGUAGE
LEARNERS:
ELEMENTARY

CHINESE STORIES
FOR LANGUAGE
LEARNERS:
INTERMEDIATE

THE ART OF WAR
FOR LANGUAGE
LEARNERS

MANADARIN
WRITING
PRACTICE BOOK

LEARN CHINESE
VOCABULARY FOR
BEGINNERS
(NEW HSK 2)

LEARN CHINESE
VOCABULARY FOR
BEGINNERS
(NEW HSK 3)

Get notified about **new releases**
https://linglingmandarin.com/notify

ABOUT THE AUTHOR

LingLing is a native Chinese Mandarin educator with an MA in Communication and Language. Originally from China, now living in the UK, she is the founder of the learning brand LingLing Mandarin, which aims to create the best resources for learners to master the Chinese language and achieve deep insight into Chinese culture in a fun and illuminating way. *Discover more about LingLing and access more great resources by following the links below or scanning the QR codes.*

 WEBSITE
linglingmandarin.com

YOUTUBE CHANNEL
youtube.com/c/linglingmandarin

 PATREON
patreon.com/linglingmandarin

INSTAGRAM
instagram.com/linglingmandarin

Printed in Great Britain
by Amazon

28119369R10090